Top 25 locator m[...]
(continues on ins[...]
back cover)
◄

CityPack
Sydney *Top 25*

ANNE MATTHEWS

If you have any comments
or suggestions for this guide
you can contact the editor at
Citypack@theAA.com

AA Publishing
Find out more about AA Publishing and the wide range
of travel publications and services the AA provides by
visiting our website at www.theAA.com/bookshop

About This Book

ORGANIZATION
This guide is divided into six chapters:
- Planning Ahead, Getting There
- Living Sydney—Sydney Now, Sydney Then, Time to Shop, Out and About, Walks, Sydney by Night
- Sydney's Top 25 Sights
- Sydney's Best—best of the rest
- Where To—detailed listings of restaurants, hotels, shops and nightlife
- Travel Facts—practical information

In addition, easy-to-read side panels provide extra facts and snippets, highlights of places to visit and invaluable practical advice.

The colours of the tabs on the page corners match the colours of the triangles aligned with the chapter names on the contents page opposite.

MAPS
The fold-out map in the wallet at the back of this book is a comprehensive street plan of Sydney. The first (or only) grid reference given for each attraction refers to this map. **The Top 25 locator map** found on the inside front and back covers of the book itself is for quick reference. It shows the Top 25 Sights, described on pages 26–50, which are clearly plotted by number (**1**–**25**, not page number) in the author's suggested viewing order. The second map reference given for the Top 25 Sights refers to this map.

Contents

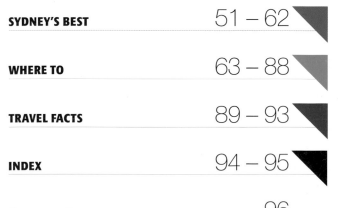

Planning Ahead

WHEN TO GO

Sydney's tourist months are December to January. March and April or September and October are better times to visit, as the crowds have thinned and the weather is warm and sunny. Take an umbrella as—subtropical thunderstorms are common.

TIME

Sydney is 9 hours ahead of the UK, 14 hours ahead of New York and 17 hours ahead of Los Angeles.

AVERAGE DAILY MAXIMUM TEMPERATURES

JAN	FEB	MAR	APR	MAY	JUN	JUL	AUG	SEP	OCT	NOV	DEC
79°F	79°F	77°F	72°F	66°F	63°F	61°F	64°F	68°F	72°F	75°F	77°F
26°C	26°C	25°C	22°C	19°C	17°C	16°C	18°C	20°C	22°C	24°C	25°C

Spring (September to November) is warm with sunny days that are mostly dry; the nights are cool to mild.

Summer (December to February) is warm to very hot but can also be humid and rather wet. Thunderstorms are common.

Autumn (March to May) sees mild to warm days with mild to cool nights. This season is generally dry.

Winter (June to August) is mostly dry with mild, sunny days and cool nights. Take a medium-weight coat.

WHAT'S ON

January *Festival of Sydney*: A month-long celebration.
International cricket matches: Sydney Cricket Ground.
Australia Day (26 Jan): The nation celebrates its birthday with fireworks.
February *Chinese New Year*: Fireworks and feasting in Chinatown.
Tropfest: Outdoor short-film festival.
March *Gay and Lesbian Mardi Gras*: The city's biggest street parade.
March/April *The Golden Slipper*: A popular horse race.
Anzac Day (25 Apr):

War Veterans Parade.
Royal Easter Show: Agriculture show, Sydney Showground.
May *Sydney Writers' Festival*: National and international speakers.
June *Sydney Film Festival*: Films from many nations.
August *City-to-Surf*: A 14-km (9-mile) run to Bondi Beach.
September *Rugby Grand Finals*: League and union teams battle it out in their respective finals.
October *Manly Jazz Festival*: Music by the sea.
November *Melbourne Cup* (1st Tue): The country's top

horse race brings the nation to a halt for 15 minutes.
December *Sydney to Hobart Race* (26 Dec): A spectacular start to one of the world's great yacht races.

Listings Check the entertainment pages of the *Sydney Morning Herald*. On Fridays this newspaper publishes the 20-page *Metro* guide, detailing everything from opera to free outdoor events. Other useful free publications are *This Week in Sydney* and *What's On in Sydney*, available from hotels and tourist kiosks.

SYDNEY ONLINE
At the heart of Australia's digital culture, Sydney has excellent websites with regularly updated information on everything from the theatre to local news, weather and gossip, as well as listings of hotels and restaurants.

www.sydney.com.au
www.sydney.citysearch.com.au
Professional reviews of shops, restaurants, nightspots, museums, cinema, theatres and much more.

www.eventwatch.com.au
A good site for events and festivals.

www.sydneyoperahouse.com
Look here for listings of performances and events on-line at the Sydney Opera House, with a booking option and a virtual tour.

www.australia.com
The official site of the Australian Tourist Commission.

www.tourism.nsw.gov.au
A complete guide with travel information, and listings of hotels and events in Sydney and New South Wales.

www.discoversydney.com.au
General information for Sydney. Includes population figures, location and climate.

www.thisweekinaustralia.com
General information on attractions, shopping, events and dining.

www.sydneyairport.com.au
A valuable site for flight information and all you need to know at the airport including hotels and duty-free shopping.

www.smh.com.au
The *Sydney Morning Herald's* own website gives up-to-date information on dining, nightlife and events news.

GOOD TRAVEL SITES

www.fodors.com
A travel-planning site where you can research prices and weather; book tickets, cars and rooms; and link to other sites.

www.131500.com.au
Timetables, routes and fares for buses, trains and ferries.

www.cityofsydney.nsw.gov.au
Practical tips on the city and what's on information.

CYBERCAFÉS

PhoneNetCafé
Internet, snacks and coffee.
✚ off map to east
✉ 73 Hall Street, Bondi
☎ 9365 0861 ◷ Daily 8am–10pm

Global Gossip
Internet, inexpensive phone calls; discounts for all Global Gossip outlets.
✚ L6 ✉ 111 Darlinghurst Rd, Kings Cross ☎ 9326 9777
◷ Daily 8am–midnight

Well-Connected Internet Café
Internet, snacks available.
✚ H7 ✉ 35 Glebe Point Road, Glebe ☎ 9566 2655
◷ Daily 7am–10pm

5

Getting There

ENTRY REQUIREMENTS

All visitors to Australia require a valid passport and an Electronic Travel Authority (ETA), which has replaced the traditional visa.

A Tourist ETA is valid for multiple travel within one year (or the expiry date of your passport, if sooner) on three-month visits. An ETA is available through most travel agents, as well as overseas Australian diplomatic offices.

MONEY

The Australian unit of currency is the Australian dollar ($), comprising 100 cents. Banknotes come in denominations of 100, 50, 20, 10 and 5 dollars. Coins come in 5, 10, 20 and 50 cents (silver), and 1 and 2 dollars (gold-coloured).

$10

$20

$50

$100

ARRIVING

Sydney International Airport is the main port of entry. The airport is 11km (7 miles) from the city centre. There are numerous daily flights, buses and train services to Sydney from all major towns and cities in Australia.

FROM SYDNEY INTERNATIONAL AIRPORT
For airport information contact ☎ 9667 9111; www.sydneyairport.com.au

Cityrail trains take 15 minutes from the airport to central Sydney and cost $11 each way.

The Kingsford Smith Transport/Sydney Airporter bus (☎ 9666 9988; website as for Sydney airport) operates every 20–30 minutes to all hotels, bed-and-breakfasts and backpackers hostels, in the Kings Cross, city and Darling Harbour areas. Cost is $8 and $13 for a round trip .

A taxi from the airport into the city takes about 20 minutes and costs around $30.

ARRIVING BY BUS
Greyhound Australia (☎ 13 1499) into the city terminate at Central Station, Eddy Avenue side.

ARRIVING BY TRAIN
CountryLink (☎ 13 2232) rail services from state destinations terminate at Central Railway south of central Sydney.

GETTING AROUND:

Sydney is compact and much of it can be explored on foot. But taxis are plentiful. The city has a good transit system of buses and ferries, as well a partly underground city and suburban rail system (☎ 13 1500). Free public transport maps are available from bus, ferry and train offices at Circular Quay, Wynyard bus station and Town Hall train station. A monorail links the city centre with Darling Harbour, Chinatown, Sydney Aquarium, the National Maritime Museum and the Powerhouse Museum (every few minutes, daily 7am–midnight).

A light rail service connects Central Station to Chinatown, Darling Harbour, StarCity Casino and the Sydney Fish Market. Sydney's inter-city rail services include the City Circle (Central, Town Hall, Wynard, Circular Quay, St. James and Museum) and the Eastern Suburbs Line.

Sydney's buses are blue and white. The most important bus stations are Circular Quay (to Bondi Beach, the eastern suburbs, the south and some inner-west areas) and Wynyard (over Harbour Bridge). Ordinary tickets can be purchased on board, but multi-trip passes should be bought from the driver or State Transit sales outlets. Exact change is necessary on the bus and bus passes slot into a machine at the front of the bus.

Ferry services operate from four wharves on Circular Quay to 30 places around the harbour, including Manly and Taronga Zoo, and up-river to Homebush Bay and Parramatta. You can buy tickets from the Circular Quay counters opposite Wharf 4.

Water taxis operate to and from virtually anywhere on the harbour that has steps or a wharf.

Rental car operators offer various deals for short- or long-term car rental. You must be over 21 and have a home country or international driver's licence.

For more public transport details (► 91–92).

INSURANCE

Check your policy and buy any necessary supplements. It is vital that travel insurance covers medical expenses, in addition to accident, trip cancellation, baggage loss and theft. Check the policy covers any continuing treatment for a chronic condition.

VISITORS WITH DISABILITIES

Most of Sydney's attractions are suitable for visitors using a wheelchair, with ramped public buildings and accessible buses, ferries, rail stations and taxis. Some hotels have roll-in showers, and some have Braille signage. For details, check out www.dirc.asn.au. Older buildings are often retrofitted with ramped access and many National Trust properties are at least partially accessible. Many Sydney attractions have hearing loops. You'll usually find parking places for drivers with disabilities, although you'll need a temporary permit from the Roads and Traffic Authority to use them (☎ 13 2213).

living
Sydney

Sydney Now

Above: *Ice-skating in Macquire Centre*
Centre top: *Yacht sailing under Sydney Harbour Bridge*
Centre bottom: *Ferry sailing near Sydney Harbour Bridge on Circular Quay*

Sydney is an easy place to get know and like. Cosmopolitan, diverse, energetic and easygoing, it's blessed with a long, sheltered harbour and a sunny, subtropical climate. It has colonial heritage, dazzling modern buildings and a free-wheeling lifestyle. It's clean, unpolluted and relatively safe. No wonder people who live here think it's the best address on earth. Nor is it surprising that it's most often classed as one of the world's most liveable cities.

Skyscrapers punctuate the skyline, the result of the lifting of height restrictions in the Central Business

DISTRICTS

• Sydney's sprawling neighbourhoods are bounded on the south, west and north by mountains and by the Pacific Ocean on its east. Sydney Harbour and the Parramatta River bisect the city laterally, dividing leafy northern areas such as Lane Cove, North Sydney and Mosman and northern beach areas like Manly, Avalon and Palm Beach, from the southern and eastern neighbourhoods such as Rockdale, Bondi and Vaucluse. To the west are Parrametta, Liverpool and a series of new housing estates stretching to Penrith, at the foot of the Blue Mountains. Around the city centre are several other vibrant areas. Darlinghurst, Kings Cross and Paddington just to the east of the CBD are popular for dining and nightlife, and Glebe, Balmain, Leichardt and Newton in the inner west are excellent for international cuisine and shopping.

Above: *Singing carols in the Domain*
Left: *Sydney skyline from Dover Heights*

OLYMPIC SUCCESS

- Called the best Games ever by the IOC, Sydney staged an Olympic exhibition that wowed the world. For a nation of sports lovers, it was not only an opportunity to show off its talent but also a time to show the world how the country has come of age. With stunning opening and closing ceremonies and a swag of gold medals for local athletes, Sydney proved that the Olympic spirit was alive and well Down Under.

District (CBD), while the forces of conservation have moved to preserve the reminders of the city's past elsewhere, most notably structures in Macquarie Street and The Rocks, but also Victorian-era buildings such as the Town Hall and the Queen Victoria Building. As host venue for the 2000 Olympic Games Sydney shone, after the city undertook still further new building and restoration projects.

Far from being the clichéd sun, sand, surf and sport scene you might expect, Sydney also has world-class museums and galleries as well as a roster of shops that include branches of world-renowned stores such as Tiffany and Cartier. The

11

Above: *Breakfast at Bondi Beach*
Right: *Doyles restaurant on Watsons Bay*

VITAL STATISTICS

- From the 1,400 people who arrived on the fleet, Sydney's population has grown to 3.9 million.

- Sydney is 15,470km (9,615 miles) from New York and 16,580km (10,305 miles) from London (via Singapore).

- Around 70 per cent of Sydneysiders are a combination of at least two ethnic backgrounds, while 36 per cent are foreign-born.

cuisine is excellent—Sydney is now one of the modern food capitals of the world. And some of the finest wines on earth come from Australia's many vineyards. After dark you can take in an opera or ballet at the Sydney Opera House, see a first-class theatrical production, dance the night away in a classy pub, take in the sparkling vistas from a vantage point such as Sydney Tower, or spend the evening sampling local beer in a historic sandstone hotel at Sydney's birthplace, The Rocks.

The pace in Sydney is faster than in other parts of Australia, so the nasally Australian English with its distinctive colloquialisms—'Strine' as it's known—is delivered double time. But Australians in general are relaxed and easygoing, and that's true in Sydney as well. Sydneysiders go about life as if there's no tomorrow. The often-heard expressions 'No worries, mate' and 'She'll be right' say much about the attitudes here. Littered streets, rude,

overstressed people and formality are not in evidence. Australians are often cheerfully laid back.

Above: *Christmas lights, North Ryde*

The great irony of this city of freedom is that it started life as a penal settlement for Britain's overcrowded prisons and a place where the poor could start afresh. Far from the limitations of England, these reluctant pioneers laid the foundations for a new society that could simply invent itself.

Today's society embraces people of all races and nationalities and, although this certainly isn't a

TETSUYA WAKUDA

• Japanese-born Tetsuya Wakuda, founder and chef at Tetsuya's, has kept his establishment at the top of the competitive Sydney restaurant scene for over 10 years with a set 12-course menu that crosses Japanese cuisine with French and Australian. So, although he is unconcerned with promoting himself (unlike many celebrity chefs) it's impossible to get a table at his 80-seat restaurant in Kent Street, unless you reserve weeks in advance.

FAMOUS SYDNEYSIDERS

• For many, being famous at home is not good enough; heading overseas to hit the big time is an Australian tradition. So people are among Sydney's most famous exports–among them supermodel Elle Macpherson, actors, Mel Gibson, Nicole Kidman and Cate Blanchett, author and TV personality Clive James, and art critic Robert Hughes.

13

Above: *Surfing on Bondi Beach*
Above right: *Chinese New Year in Chinatown*

multicultural utopia, the principals of the once racist White Australia laws have long been buried. While few Aboriginal people live in Sydney, Asian faces can be seen everywhere and you might find

THE DIASPORA

• With all the publicity given to Australia's immigration agendas and its multicultural mix, it comes as a surprise to many when they hear that nearly one million Australians—five per cent of the population—live and/or work in other countries. In the past, the scattering of one people all over the world—a diaspora—has been seen as a negative, but overseas Australians are an important resource for Australia. Expatriates have been quiet achievers in Asian countries such as Singapore for many years and the professions and services made more dynamic by communications technology have stimulated the trend to work abroad. Far from this being a 'brain drain'— Australia still manages a net inflow of skilled workers— the diaspora actually promotes Australia's cultural and commercial interests overseas. And when these people return, as they most often do, they bring new skills and new perspectives to their workplace.

yourself inadvertently eavesdropping on conversations in Italian, Lebanese, Japanese or Vietnamese. While world events may have turned people somewhat inward, and a conservative national government reversed a long-established open policy on refugees, Sydneysiders remain friendly and open.

Come to Sydney with an open mind, meet them halfway, take Sydney as it comes, and you're bound to have a relaxing good time.

ABORIGINAL PRESENCE

• Aboriginals have lived on the Australian mainland for over 40,000 years, and many of their descendants can be found in Sydney, particularly in the suburbs of Redfern and La Perouse. Although shops nationwide are full of arts and crafts from Aboriginal artisans, all that remains of Aboriginal culture in the Sydney region are shell middens on the harbour foreshores, rock-carvings in surrounding national parks and original settlement place-names such as Woolloomooloo, Maroubra, Turramurra and Parramatta.

DID YOU KNOW?

• Work began on Sydney Harbour Bridge in 1923. The bridge opened in March 1932.

• Australia's national airline, Qantas, began scheduled flights between Sydney and London in 1934.

• Queen Elizabeth opened Sydney Opera House in 1973.

• Sydney Harbour Tunnel opened in 1992, relieving the Harbour Bridge of some of its traffic.

• Chinese, in its various forms, is Sydney's second language.

15

Sydney Then

Above: *Emigrants arriving at Sydney Harbour in 17th century*
Above right: *Building of the Sydney Harbour Bridge, close to completion (1932)*

THE FIRST FLEET

The most bizarre birth of any nation on earth might so easily have been a disastrous false start, but Sydney and the nation have thrived, thanks initially to Governor Phillip and the people who travelled on the First Fleet of 11 ships from England. These reluctant pioneers of 1788–including 568 male and 191 female convicts, and 200 marines and their wives and children–suffered incredible hardships to set this isolated colony on its feet. For the first two years, lack of farming skills meant near starvation, and it was only the fortuitous arrival of supply ships from England that saved the day.

40,000– 50,000BC Aborigines arrive from Southeast Asia.

29 Apr AD1770 Captain James Cook and the crew of the *Endeavour* arrive at Botany Bay.

1779 Suggestions are made in England that New South Wales could become a penal colony.

13 May 1787 The First Fleet sails from Portsmouth, England. The 11 ships carry more than 1,400 people.

20 Jan 1788 The First Fleet arrives at Botany Bay. The commander and first governor of the colony, Captain Arthur Phillip, deems the site unsuitable and moves his settlement north to Port Jackson (Sydney Harbour). The colony of New South Wales is proclaimed.

1793 The first free settlers land in Sydney.

1804 An uprising of 400 Irish convicts occurs at Castle Hill. Australia's second settlement is founded at Hobart, Tasmania.

1813 A route over the impenetrable Blue Mountains is finally discovered by explorers Wentworth, Lawson and Blaxland, opening up Australia's agricultural potential.

1832 Assisted passages over the next 140 years help millions of people, mainly Britons, to emigrate to Australia.

1840 Convict transportation to New South Wales ends.

1851 Gold is discovered near Bathurst, and Sydney's population doubles in 10 years.

1900 Bubonic plague breaks out in The Rocks.

1901 The Commonwealth of Australia is proclaimed at Centennial Park on 1 January, joining the six Australian colonies into a federation.

1939–45 Australian troops fight overseas during World War II.

1947 Post-war immigration from Europe begins, boosting skilled labour.

1992 The 150th anniversary of Sydney's city status.

1999 Australia votes against becoming a republic.

2000 Sydney hosts the Olympic Games.

2003 Australian troops join US forces in the war on Iraq.

Above left: *Sydney hosted the Olympics in 2000*
Above: *John Howard, prime minister of Australia, set for a record time in office*

GOLD FEVER

Although declared a city in 1842, it was not until the 1851 discovery of gold near Bathurst, beyond the Blue Mountains, that Sydney really came of age. Word soon spread and prospectors arrived from all over the world and Sydney boomed, with the population virtually doubling in a decade.

17

Time to Shop

Apart from having the usual swag of international brand-name retail outlets, Sydney has many shops selling designer clothing, original arts and crafts and stunning gemstone

Stall selling didgeridoos at The Rocks market

jewellery. Travellers keen to take home a memento generally go for an item of Australiana such as diamond, opal or pearl jewellery (► 75); Akubra stockmen's hats; outback clothing; Drizabone rainware; kangaroo or crocodile leather products; or exquisite craft objects in glass, wood, porcelain and silver inspired by Australian nature (► 74).

The range of Aboriginal arts and crafts is enormous. But try to distinguish between hand-made craft items derived from distinct Aboriginal settlements from the mundane, generic goods that are mass produced and have no authenticity. Look out for the signed traditional bowls, digeridoos, boomerangs and wood carvings. Art enthusiasts go for the Arnhen Land bark paintings and Central Australian dot paintings. Seek out a reputable gallery and ask questions regarding provenance and authenticity.

Original Australian design brands to look out for include Ken Done (► 74), featuring bright,

MUSEUM SHOPS

At the Art Gallery of New South Wales, you'll find Sydney's best selection of art books and cards.

The Museum of Contemporary Art offers jewellery, design objects and books inspired by Australian designers.

The Australian Museum shop focuses on Australian nature books.

The Australian Centre for Photography showcases local talent.

vibrant clothing, homewares, bags, prints and jewellery and Mambo (► 74) with surf and streetwear featuring funky designs. There are several local store chains selling goods that are

Middle: *Hats for sale at Oxford Street market*
Left: *Armani store on Elizabeth Street*

not found internationally, including The Australian Geographic Shop (► 74), offering environmentally friendly goods, Australian nature books and outdoor clothing and the ABC Shop, operated by the Australian Broadcasting Corporation, selling books, audio and video products, and toys relating to popular local TV shows.

Those who have sampled the widely exported Aussie wines will be impressed with the huge range on offer. While the major grape varieties from regions such as the Hunter Barossa and Yarra Valleys are well known, look for Margaret River and Clare Valley wines; also check out the newest grape varieties Verdelho and Petit Verdo.

And finally, if you must impress friends back home with an item not found elsewhere, pick up a Macadamia nut cracker. Normally sold with a bunch of nuts to crack, this threaded screw device cracks the shells of Australia's major contribution to the world's food stocks.

AUSTRALIAN GEMS AND JEWELLERY

Sydney is internationally renowned for the range and quality of opal, pearl and other gemstone jewellery. The best shops feature original designs utilizing multi-hued opals, lustrous South Sea pearls and exquisite Argyle diamonds in white, pink and champagane shades. You can also buy loose stones, especially opals; the high quality Australian varieties are recognized as some of the best in the world. You can purchase such stones and jewellery tax free. The value of an opal is judged by the depth of colour. Red is the most prized, followed by orange, yellow, green, blue, indigo and violet. Buy only solid opals, not inferior doublets or triplets. South Sea pearls are graded by lustre, colour, size, shape, surface perfection and rarity. For shops selling such stones see ► 75.

Out and About

ORGANIZED SIGHTSEEING

Below: *The revolving restaurants atop Sydney's AMP Tower*
Below right: *Royal Botanic Gardens, Sydney Tropical Centre*

If your time is limited, opt for a guided bus tour. Sydney Day Tours (☎ 9251 6101) has half-day and full-day tours of the city and the surrounding area, including wildlife parks. Captain Cook Cruises (☎ 9206 1122) offers day and night harbour cruises.

WALKING TOURS

The Rocks Walking Tours (☎ 9247 6678) conducts small escorted groups around the historic Rocks and Miller's Point, Circular Quay, the Opera House, The Royal Botanic Gardens, Macquarie Street, Bridge Street and Macquarie Place.

Walks Around Sydney (☎ 9247 9854) offers three different tours, including an icons tour, a maritime tour and an Aboriginal history tour.

ITINERARIES

THE ROCKS TO SYDNEY TOWER

Start at The Rocks (➤ 30) and walk to the Museum of Contemporary Art (➤ 42). Catch a bus along George Street to the Town Hall and the city centre (➤ 35). Look around the Victorian-era Queen Victoria Building (➤ 34) and take a break in one of the Pitt Street Mall cafes. Take the high-speed elevators to the top of Sydney Tower for city views. Walk to Macquarie Street, where there are many interesting colonial buildings (➤ 35).

CHINATOWN TO DARLING HARBOUR

Start the day in Chinatown (➤ 40), where you can stroll and browse in the shops. Tour the nearby Chinese Gardens, then head to the Powerhouse Museum (➤ 36). Walk to the Sydney Aquarium (➤ 31). In Darling Harbour there's an abundance of restaurants and entertainment at Harbourside Shopping Centre and Sydney's newest eating precinct, Cockle Bay, a converted three-tiered former wharf complex. The National Maritime Museum (➤ 39) and Star City Casino are nearby.

EXCURSIONS
BLUE MOUNTAINS

Cooler than Sydney in summer and bracingly cold in winter, the Blue Mountains are famous for their good hotels, excellent restaurants and grand scenery. People flock to mountain towns like Springwood, Leura, Katoomba, Wentworth Falls,

Blackheath and Mt. Victoria to take in the views, walk the trails, shop for arts, crafts and antiques and generally enjoy the mountain air. A variety of superb temperate climate gardens are open for inspection, and the cool-climate annex of the Royal Botanic Gardens at Mt. Tomah is brilliantly hued in autumn and a mass of flowers in the spring and summer.

HUNTER VALLEY

Wine lovers enjoy the trip to the historic Hunter Valley vineyards, just three hours north of Sydney, near the old coal mining town of Cessnock. A good selection of bus tours is available from Sydney and, given the nature of the main activity here, may be the preferred means of travel. A well-established circuit travels past the cellar doors of dozens of wineries, where you are encouraged to sample the different products and may be invited to meet and observe the winemakers in their cellars. There are many fine restaurants in the area where you can buy a good meal accompanied by some excellent local wines.

INFORMATION

BLUE MOUNTAINS
Distance 58km (36 miles) from Sydney to Katoomba
🚉 From Central Station, approximately 2 hours
ℹ️ Blue Mountain's Visitor Centres: Glenbrook Tourist Information Centre, Great Western Highway, Glenbrook
☎ 02 4739 6266;
Katoomba Tourist Information Centre, Echo Point Road, Katoomba
☎ 02 4739 6266,
Blue Mountain Heritage Centre, Govetts Leap Road, Blackheath
☎ 02 4739 6266

The vineyards of Mount Pleasant in the Hunter Valley produce some of Australia's best wines

INFORMATION

HUNTER VALLEY
Journey Time Bus trip takes 3 hours
🚌 Bus from Sydney
Distance 120km (72 miles) each way
ℹ️ Hunter Valley Tourist Information Centre www.huntervalleyinfo.com.au
Cessnock Tourist Information Centre Turner Park, Aberdare Road, Cessnock
☎ 02 4990 4477, www.winecountry.com.au

Walks

INFORMATION

Distance 4km (2.5 miles)
Time 2 hours (plus visits to Opera House and Art Gallery)
Start point ★ Circular Quay
🚌 bii; J5
🚉 Circular Quay
End point Circular Quay
🍴 Pack a picnic to eat in the Royal Botanic Gardens or stop at the Art Gallery café.

Looking across Circular Quay to the Sydney Opera House and Harbour Bridge

CIRCULAR QUAY TO NSW ART GALLERY

Start your walk from the ferry terminals at Circular Quay (► 29) and follow the water's edge to the Opera House (► 26) for some of the best views back to the city and towards the Harbour Bridge (► 27). At the Opera House, climb the steps in front and take a guided tour. Walk to Bennelong Point at ground level to watch the passing water-traffic.

Enter the Royal Botanic Gardens at the gate adjacent to the Opera House, and walk along the water around Farm Cove for a way before detouring along the garden pathways to see the various plant displays and specimens. Don't miss the tropical plant pyramids at the Macquarie Street end and the visitor centre (next to Mrs Macquaries Road), where exhibitions of a botanical nature are often held. Return to the water's edge and exit the Gardens to check the views from the point at Mrs Macquaries Chair.

Map of Sydney Cove, Circular Quay

Allow plenty of time at the nearby Art Gallery of New South Wales (► 45), to view the Australian, Asian and European works of art. The excellent Yiribana Gallery of Aboriginal Art, the most recent addition to the complex, showcases more than 200 items.

Paddington and Woollahra

Paddington and Woollahra grew up around the 1841 Victoria Barracks (➤ 57) and by the 1880s was crammed with terraced (row) houses. With their iron lacework balconies, the brick-built terraces make Paddington unique and charming.

From the top of Oxford Street, turn left onto Queen Street, full of exclusive antiques shops. Take a left onto Moncur Street and walk down Hargrave Street; you are now in the conservation area of Paddington listed by the National Trust. Turn left onto Elizabeth Street, right to Paddington Street and right again onto Cascade Street, which has some particularly good examples of the local architecture, made in the local sandstone material.

Walk down Cascade Street, head left onto Gurner Street and continue along Glenmore Road to Five Ways. Approximately 200m (180 yards) further along Glenmore Road, turn left onto steep Ormond Street, with more old terraced houses. Back on Oxford Street, turn left to reach the main Paddington shopping and café strip, home of Sydney's most interesting clothing shops as well as book, music and jewellery outlets and the Saturday Paddington Bazaar is held here (➤ 76).

INFORMATION

Distance 3km (2 miles)
Time 45 minutes–2 hours
Start point ★ Corner of Queen and Oxford streets
➕ M8
▣ 378, 380
End point Oxford Street–main shopping/café area between William Street and Jersey Road
➕ L8

Paddington Bazaar

23

Sydney Opera House

HIGHLIGHTS

- Location on Bennelong Point
- Ceramic-tiled roof
- Concert Hall
- Opera Theatre
- *Five Bells* mural, by Australian artist John Olsen
- *Possum Dreaming* mural

INFORMATION

www.sydneyoperahouse.com
- ci; K4
- Bennelong Point
- Tours 9250 7250.
  Box office 9250 7777
- Tours daily 8.30–4.
  Performances most days.
  Closed Good Fri, 25 Dec
- Four restaurants and cafés
- Circular Quay
- Sydney Explorer
- Circular Quay
- Good
- Moderate
- Sydney Harbour (➤ 28),
  Circular Quay (➤ 29),
  The Rocks (➤ 30),
  Museum of
  Contemporary Art
  (➤ 42), Royal Botanic
  Gardens & The Domain
  (➤ 44), Museum of
  Sydney (➤ 46)
- Tours daily; free outdoor concerts

This once controversial, yet ethereal, sail-roofed building rising from the water on its prominent harbourside site, epitomizes the free-spirited nature of this young and vibrant harbour city.

Sydney's most recognizable building The opera house was conceived by Danish architect Joern Utzon, who won a design competition in 1959. It took 14 years to create this masterpiece, which was opened in 1973 by Queen Elizabeth II, although the project was fraught with technical and political problems and Utzon eventually resigned. The building holds four performance halls—for theatre, dance, symphony concerts, opera and other events—restaurants and bars, and a maze of backstage areas. It also houses the Performing Arts Library and Archives. The roofs are covered with more than a million ceramic tiles, and the vast stone base and terraces are modelled on the Mayan and Aztec temples of Mexico. You can enjoy the exterior at any time; a walk around gives you a chance to view the building from many perspectives.

The interior While the architect's vision for the interior was never fully realized, there is much to

see here including a John Olsen mural, *Salute to Five Bells*, in the northern foyer of the Concert Hall, and a Michael Tjakamarra mural, titled *Possum Dreaming*, in the foyer of the Opera Theatre. If possible, attend a performance or take a guided tour to fully appreciate this place.

Sydney Harbour Bridge

Affectionately called 'the coat hanger' by locals, the Sydney Harbour Bridge is one of the most famous symbols of this city. Take a climb to the top of the bridge for great harbour views.

All things to all people This bridge is an essential link between the south and north sides of the harbour, the perfect postcard backdrop to the Opera House, and a great spot to take in the harbour panorama. The world's widest long-span bridge was opened in March 1932, and is 50m (1,360ft) long and 49m (130ft) wide, with eight road lanes, two railway tracks, a cycleway and a footpath. Crossing by car, bus or train just isn't the same— by far the best experience is walking across. From the city side, access to the walkway is via Argyle Street in The Rocks, while the northern entrance is near Milsons Point station; a ferry service operates between Milsons Point and Circular Quay. Bridge Climb (► 60) runs a three-hour climb to the top of the bridge's arch.

The Pylon Lookout The highlight of a walk across the bridge is a stop at the southeast pylon. There is an interesting display here on how the bridge was constructed, and the 200-step climb to the lookout is well worthwhile, for the views of the harbour and the city are magnificent.

HIGHLIGHTS

- The walk across
- View from the Pylon Lookout
- Pylon Lookout display
- Close-up look at the structure
- Climb to the top of the bridge

INFORMATION

www.sydney.com.au/bridge.htm
- ➕ J4
- ✉ Pylon Lookout
- ☎ 9247 3408
- 🕐 Daily 10–5; closed 25 Dec
- 🚉 Circular Quay (southern side)
- 🚌 Sydney Explorer
- 🚉 Milsons Point (northern side)
- ⛴ Circular Quay (southern side)
- 💲 Walkway free. Pylon Lookout inexpensive
- 🔗 Mary McKillop Museum (► 54), Sydney Opera House (► 26), Circular Quay (► 29), The Rocks (► 30), Sydney Observatory (► 50)

Sydney Harbour

HIGHLIGHTS

- Ferry ride or cruise
- Fort Denison
- Views from South Head and North Head
- Goat Island
- The Spit to Manly walk (➤ 53)
- Picnic on Shark Island

INFORMATION

www.shfa.nsw.gov.au

➕ L4

✉ Fort Denison, Sydney Harbour

☎ 9240 8500

🕐 Tours daily from Circular Quay

🚉 Circular Quay

🚌 Sydney Explorer to Circular Quay

⛴ From Circular Quay

↔ Sydney Opera House (➤ 26), Sydney Harbour Bridge (➤ 27), Circular Quay (➤ 29), The Rocks (➤ 30), Royal Botanic Gardens & The Domain (➤ 44)

🅿 For guided tours and cruises to Goat Island and Fort Denison, contact National Parks ☎ 9247 5033

Spectacular Sydney Harbour, officially Port Jackson, undoubtedly makes this city special. You get stunning water views from the most unexpected places and the still waters are a wonderful place for sailing and swimming. Be sure to take a ferry ride to Manly.

Sydney Harbour With a shoreline that stretches for 240km (149 miles), Sydney's harbour is guaranteed to delight. The best way to enjoy this setting is to take a ferry ride or cruise (➤ 20), most of which depart from Circular Quay; you can travel on anything from a square-rigged schooner to a high-speed JetCat. You can visit beautiful Cremorne Point, Taronga Zoo (➤ 38), Manly (➤ 37) and Watsons Bay (➤ 53), or take an evening cruise to view the spectacular city lights. Harbourside walks, such as those around North Head or South Head, are also popular, while Sydney Harbour National Park (➤ 53) encompasses Shark, Clark, Goat and Rodd islands, which can be toured or reserved for picnics (➤ panel). After you have taken in the more obvious attractions of the main part of the harbour, head west beyond the Harbour Bridge or take a RiverCat trip upriver to Parramatta or Homebush Bay, or travel by ferry to the suburbs of Balmain, Birchgrove, Greenwich, Hunters Hill and Meadowbank.

Fort Denison This harbour island was once known as 'Pinchgut', after the practice of marooning disobedient convicts here with extremely meager rations. By 1857, the island had become Fort Denison, constructed to defend Sydney against possible Russian invasion during the Crimean War.

Circular Quay

The focal point of Sydney's maritime life since European settlement, Circular Quay is today a bustling pedestrian precinct with ferry, bus and rail terminals. Be sure to check out the galleries, stores and restaurants in nearby Customs House.

HIGHLIGHTS

- Customs House
- Ferry terminal
- Cadman's Cottage
- Writers Walk
- Buskers
- Harbour views
- Galleries

INFORMATION

www.sydney.com.au/
quay htm
- J5
- Circular Quay
- Customs House
  information line 9265
  9189
- Daily; closed Good Fri,
  25 Dec
- Cafés and restaurants
- Circular Quay
- Various
- Moderate
- Sydney Opera House
  (► 26), Sydney Harbour
  (► 28), The Rocks
  (► 30), City Centre
  (► 35), Museum of
  Contemporary Art
  (► 42)

Circular Quay The city's ferry terminal is a great place to sit and watch the boats and buskers, or enjoy a coffee. The covered walkway from the Opera House includes Writers Walk, with plaques that commemorate some prominent Australian authors, poets and playwrights.

Circular Quay West The surrounding precinct of Circular Quay West contains Cadman's Cottage, the city's oldest building (1816). It is now a National Parks and Wildlife information centre (☎ 9247 5033). Also in this area is First Fleet Park, commemorating the nation's first settlers, and the large Overseas Passenger Terminal.

Customs House From 1845 to 1990 this was home to the Customs Service, but today the building's interior has been refurbished as a major cultural venue. Included here are galleries, cafés, studios and a performance space.

The International Passenger Terminal at Circular Quay

The Rocks

HIGHLIGHTS

- Campbells Cove
- Suez Canal and Nurses Walk
- Weekend Rocks Market (➤ 76)
- Views from Dawes Point Park

INFORMATION

www.rocksvillage.com

☷ bi; J4–J5

✉ The Rocks Heritage & Visitor Centre, 106 George Street

☎ 9255 1788

🕐 Daily 9–5

🍴 Many cafés and restaurants nearby

🚉 Circular Quay

🚌 Sydney Explorer, 431, 432, 433

🚆 Circular Quay

♿ Generally good

🆓 Free

🔀 Sydney Harbour Bridge (➤ 27), Sydney Harbour (➤ 28), Circular Quay (➤ 29), Museum of Contemporary Art (➤ 42), Sydney Observatory (➤ 50)

❓ Rocks walking tours start from the Heritage & Visitor's Centre

The district known as The Rocks, Sydney's first 'village', has a fascinating history as a colonial port area. Many of the restored old buildings now house interesting shops and galleries.

A Rocky Start Named after the rocky shore where convict tents were erected in January 1788, The Rocks is Sydney's most intriguing and picturesque area. It was once the province of seamen and traders, thieves and prostitutes, and the scene of a 1900 outbreak of bubonic plague that claimed over 100 lives. More destruction was wreaked during the 1920s, as entire streets were demolished in order to make way for the southern approach to the Harbour Bridge. Meticulous and detailed restoration since 1970, however, has transformed the district into Sydney's tourist hub, the delights of which are equally appreciated by the locals. The area is packed with a host of attractions, and these will easily fill a day—there are many 1900s buildings to admire, narrow streets such as Nurses Walk and Suez Canal to explore and plenty of shops and cafés. Campbells Cove, with its historic warehouses and Dawes Point Park under the Harbour Bridge are both good waterfront spots. As if this wasn't enough, The Rocks also offers many museums and galleries that are well worth exploring (➤ 54).

The Rocks Heritage and Visitor Centre Perhaps the best place to start your visit is at the Heritage and Visitor Centre. Housed in the restored Sailors Home built in 1864, this information and tour-booking outlet contains a shop and an illuminating upstairs display that covers the history of The Rocks. You can also take a Rocks walking tour from here.

Sydney Aquarium & Darling Harbour

Encounter sharks and crocodiles at close quarters, marvel at the species diversity of the Great Barrier Reef and explore Australia's marine environments at this world-class aquarium.

Aquatic Fun The real thrill here is walking through transparent plastic tunnels beneath the two vast floating oceanariums, watching schools of magnificent tropical fish, rays, eels and sharks glide above you. The Great Barrier Reef display features fish and coral that are impossibly vivid, while the saltwater crocodiles are awesome. Seals frolic in the Marine Mammal Sanctuary and children are able to pick up marine creatures in the touch pool.

Darling Harbour The eastern part of Darling Harbour offers several attractions, including the Panasonic IMAX Theatre, housed in a distinctive eye-shaped building. Cockle Bay Wharf, located on the city side of Darling Harbour, is a food and entertainment precinct, offering a range of dining experiences in a relaxed environment. Pyrmont Bridge (1902), which links the two sides of Darling Harbour, is the world's oldest electrically operated swingspan bridge and is still in use.

HIGHLIGHTS

- Sharks in 'The Open Ocean'
- Great Barrier Reef display
- Saltwater crocodiles
- Touch pool
- Marine Mammal Sanctuary
- Pyrmont Bridge

INFORMATION

www.darlingharbour.com
- J6
- Sydney Aquarium: Aquarium Pier. IMAX Theatre: 491 Kent Street
- Aquarium 8251 7800. IMAX Theatre 9281 3300. Information on Darling Harbour
- Aquarium daily 9.30–9. IMAX Theatre daily 10–10
- Aquarium restaurant. IMAX Theatre Star Grill
- Town Hall
- Sydney Explorer
- Monorail to Darling Park
- Aquarium Wharf
- Very good
- Expensive
- Sydney Harbour (➤ 28), Powerhouse Museum (➤ 36), National Maritime Museum (➤ 39), Chinese Garden & Chinatown (➤ 40)

Shark encounters

Bondi Beach

HIGHLIGHTS

- Beach
- Cafés on Campbell Parade
- Exhibitions and events in Bondi Pavilion Cultural Centre
- Clifftop walk to Bronte Beach
- Golf overlooking the ocean
- Surfing

INFORMATION

www.bondibeachonline.com
- Off map to east
- Bondi Beach
- Bondi Pavilion Cultural Centre 8362 3400
- Daily 24 hours
- Cafés and restaurants
- Bondi Junction, then bus 380, 382
- Bondi & Bay Explorer, 380, 382, 389
- Generally good
- Free
- Bronte Beach (▶ 59)
- Frequent festivals, exhibitions and events

Just off Australia's most famous beach

Enjoy Sydney's outdoor life at this world-famous strip of surf and sand. Regardless of the season, join the locals as they swim, sunbathe, jog, eat, drink or simply stroll along the water's edge. *The* **place for people-watching.**

Bondi beach Summer or winter, Bondi is quintessential Sydney. This is one of the world's most famous strips of surf, sand and beach life, and there is no better way of understanding how the locals enjoy themselves than by heading down to Bondi. The Aboriginal name roughly means 'the noise of tumbling waters', a description that aptly sums up this beach and its rolling surf. Perfect for a summer sunbathing and surfing session, or a brisk winter walk along the clifftop path to Tamarama and Bronte beaches. Bondi is Sydney at its very best. In summer you are likely to witness a surf carnival or other beach event, while the Bondi Pavilion Cultural Centre often holds musical and theatrical performances and art exhibitions.

Beachside Bondi Street life is just as entertaining, with its bars, pubs and cafés, as well as a good bookshop and surf and beach clothing shops. You can even play golf overlooking the ocean at the public Bondi Golf Course. Bondi is also a great place to stay, with a growing range of accommodation to suit all budgets.

Sydney Tower & Skytour

This 305-m (1,000-foot) high structure, soaring dizzily above the city, is the best place to view Sydney's layout. The incredible panorama from the tower's viewing levels extends to the Blue Mountains on a clear day.

The structure Completed in 1981, gold-topped Sydney Tower, as it is known locally, a member of the World Federation of Great Towers, is anchored to the Centrepoint shopping complex below by 56 stabilizing cables, each of which weighs almost eight tons. Skytour, a simulated ride, is a virtual adventure through Australia's cultural history and geography. This is one of the tallest public buildings in the southern hemisphere and contains two revolving restaurants, an observation level and a coffee shop. A ride in the high-speed elevator—a journey that takes a mere 40 seconds—is an experience in itself. While here, a visit to Centrepoint is also worthwhile. This large complex has over 170 stores (mainly clothing and fashion items) on four levels, several cafés and a reasonably priced basement food court.

The views The 360-degree views are incredible, and a visit to the tower is a starting point to becoming familiar with the city's layout. You will see the harbour, beyond to the ocean, the Blue Mountains 80km (50 miles) west and south towards Botany Bay, and you can clearly see aircraft taking off and landing at the airport. The observation level features high-powered binoculars and free guided tours. There are also special glass windows for glare-free photography. The views down into the city streets are no less fascinating, and a visit after dark is magical. Try dining in one of the tower's restaurants to appreciate the glittering night-time panorama.

HIGHLIGHTS

- View of Sydney Harbour, the city buildings and south to Botany Bay
- Night views
- Revolving restaurants
- High-speed elevator
- Skytour

INFORMATION

www.sydneyskytour.com.au
- biv; J6
- 100 Market Street
- 9223 0933
- Sun–Fri 9.30am–10.30pm, Sat 9.30am–11.30pm
- Two restaurants, coffee lounge
- St. James
- Any Circular Quay-bound bus
- Good
- Moderate
- Queen Victoria Building (➤ 34), Hyde Park Barracks (➤ 47), Hyde Park (➤ 62), Martin Place (➤ 62)
- Audio and guided tours

33

Top **25**

9

Queen Victoria Building

HIGHLIGHTS

- Building's façade
- Floor tiles on the ground floor
- Central dome
- Stained-glass windows
- Replica Crown jewels display on second floor
- Chinese jade bridal carriage on second floor
- Victorian-era toilets on first floor

INFORMATION

www.qvb.com.au
- biv; J6
- Corner of George, York, Market and Druitt streets
- 9264 9209
- Daily. Shops generally 9–6
- Many food stalls, cafés and restaurants
- Town Hall
- Sydney Explorer, any Circular Quay-bound bus
- Very good
- Free
- Sydney Aquarium and Darling Harbour (➤ 31), Sydney Tower (➤ 33), City Centre (Town Hall ➤ 35)

The delightfully restored interior of Sydney's most imposing Victorian-era building prompted French fashion guru Pierre Cardin to describe the structure as 'the most beautiful shopping centre in the world.'

The building Constructed to commemorate Queen Victoria's golden jubilee and completed in 1898, the domed Romanesque-style QVB was originally used to house markets downstairs and offices upstairs. The building fell into decline during the 1960s and 1970s and there were even moves to demolish this remarkable piece of history to make way for a civic centre and underground parking lot. Fortunately, it survived and in the 1980s, courtesy of a Malaysian company, meticulous restoration transformed the seven-level sandstone structure into a historic attraction and a delightful shopping mall. Capped by a central glass dome, the 200-m (180-ft) long building, occupying an entire city block and containing over 180 shops, cafés and restaurants, features beautiful stained-glass windows, patterned floor tiles and period shades and appointments, while the four main floors are divided into elegant Victorian-fronted shops.

Shopping in the QVB Shopping in such attractive surroundings is a pleasure. The lower-level food court and ground-floor shops are more run-of-the-mill, but the upper floors contain outlets for international labels such as Ralph Lauren and Papoucci, as well as excellent local designers and a wide range of quality souvenir shops. On Victoria Walk (second floor), there is an interesting collection of historical objects. Here you can admire a replica of the British Crown jewels, an incredibly ornate Chinese jade bridal carriage, the 'Royal Clock' and a jade tree.

City Centre

Many of Sydney's colonial-era and Victorian buildings have been restored and you can walk around the city centre, with its splendid parks and malls, to view some architectural gems. Don't forget the interesting little backstreets.

Colonial and Victorian Sydney From its origins as a convict settlement, Sydney has always had fine public and commercial buildings that were progressively replaced with grander and newer versions as the years went by and the population rapidly increased. Fortunately, a few colonial buildings, such as the Hyde Park Barracks and St. James Church, remain, as do splendid examples of 19th-century architecture that were built using local sandstone. One such is the Town Hall in George Street, an elaborate 1869 building. You can look at the richly decorated vestibule and the grand hall with its powerful organ at any time, or join one of the guided tours that take place on most days. Next door is St. Andrews Cathedral, while St. Marys Cathedral is on the eastern side of Hyde Park.

Art Deco Sydney A number of buildings survive, but the Anzac War Memorial, in the southern section of Hyde Park and the Archibald Fountain, in the northern section, are the most accessible and classic of all structures from this era.

Modern Sydney While many of the city's modern structures are not considered architecturally important, some buildings are worth seeking out, including Chifley Tower at Chifley Square and the Harry Seidler-designed buildings, the MLC Centre in Martin Place and Australia Square in George Street.

HIGHLIGHTS

- Sydney Town Hall
- Harry Seidler buildings
- Hyde Park
- Hyde Park Barracks
- St. Andrews Cathedral
- Sydney Mint Museum
- Chifley Tower

INFORMATION

www.cityofsydney.nsw.gov.au
- J6
- Town Hall tours
  9231 4629
- Tours daily
- Town Hall, Museum
- Few
- Free
- Circular Quay (➤ 29), Sydney Tower (➤ 33), Australian Museum (➤ 43), Royal Botanic Gardens (➤ 44), Museum of Sydney (➤ 46), Hyde Park Barracks (➤ 47), Chifley Tower (➤ 56)

The Archibald Fountain (1932) in Hyde Park, Sydney's most central park.

Powerhouse Museum

- Decorative Arts section
- Boulton and Watt engine
- King's Cinema
- 'Space: Beyond this World'
- Transportation section
- Powerhouse Garden Restaurant

INFORMATION

www.powerhousemuseum.com

- ✚ H7
- ✉ 500 Harris Street, Ultimo
- ☎ 9217 0111
- ◷ Daily 10–5; closed 25 Dec
- 🍴 Restaurant, outdoor kiosk and tables
- 🚉 Central
- 🚌 Sydney Explorer
- 🚉 Monorail to Haymarket
- 🚢 Aquarium Wharf, Darling Harbour
- ♿ Excellent
- 💰 Moderate; free 1st Sat of every month
- ↔ Sydney Aquarium & Darling Harbour (➤ 31, 62), National Maritime Museum (➤ 39), Chinese Garden & Chinatown (➤ 40)
- ❓ Guided tours, regular films, courses and display demonstrations

Sydney's most innovative museum is housed in a cavernous old power station with modern extensions. Interactive audiovisual displays are combined with fascinating historical exhibits.

The building During the 1980s the 1899 Ultimo Power Station was transformed into Sydney's largest museum. Displays are housed in the vast boiler, turbine and engine houses, as well as the Neville Wran Building, which was inspired by grand 19th-century halls and rail stations.

The collection The award-winning museum contains much of the Museum of Applied Arts and Sciences' extensive collection, which originated in the 1880s. Grouped into five themed areas—Creativity and Australian Achievement, Decorative Arts, Everyday Life in Australia, Bringing People Together and Science, Technology and People—the contents range

from the enormous 18th-century Boulton and Watt steam engine to historic gowns, audiovisual presentations, sound effects, holograms and dozens of hands-on scientific displays. You can even sit in King's Cinema, a re-creation of a 1930s art-deco cinema and watch a silent movie, accompanied by the bells, whistles and gadgetry of an electrically and air-activated Fotoplayer. Be sure to see the Garden Restaurant, painted by the Sydney artist Ken Done.

Manly & Oceanworld

The slogan 'seven miles from Sydney and a thousand miles from care' originated in the late 1880s, when ferries greatly shortened the journey to the popular suburb of Manly. Sydneysiders have flocked here ever since.

Manly The strangely titled suburb of Manly owes its name to Governor Phillip, who remarked on the 'manly' appearance of Aborigines here in 1788. It first became a beach resort in the late 1800s, and today it's just a short ferry ride or JetCat trip from the city. In summer, Manly and its excellent beaches, such as Shelly, draw surfers—the art of surfing began here in 1915—and swimmers, but there is plenty to do here at any time. The Manly Art Gallery and Museum has a good collection, and you can stroll around the modern Manly Wharf, with over 65 shops and cafés, as well as watch free street-entertainment. Continue to North Head and visit the historic Quarantine Station, or take a bus excursion to the wonderful northern beaches, such as Palm Beach or Mona Vale.

Oceanworld A good focus for your trip to Manly is a visit to Oceanworld. This big aquarium features vibrant fish of the Great Barrier Reef, as well as corals, sharks, giant stingrays and seal shows. The sharks are hand-fed twice a day.

HIGHLIGHTS

Manly
● Main beach and Shelly Beach
● Weekend Arts and Crafts Market
● Manly Art Gallery and Museum

Oceanworld
● Great Barrier Reef display
● Seal shows
● Stingrays
● Divers hand-feeding sharks

INFORMATION

www.manlyweb.com.au
✚ Off map to northeast
✉ Oceanworld, West Esplanade, Manly
☎ 9949 2644
⊙ Daily 10–5.30; closed 25 Dec
🍴 Café
🚇 Manly
♿ Few
💷 Moderate
↔ Sydney Harbour (► 28), North Head (► 53), The Spit to Manly Walk (► 53), Quarantine Station (► 55)
❓ Guided tours, special aquarium shows and various Manly events and festivals (for information ☎ 9977 1088)

Manly's amusement park

Taronga Zoo

HIGHLIGHTS

- Western Lowland gorillas
- 'Koala Walkabout' and
- photos with the koalas
- Snow leopards
- Seal shows
- 'Orang-utan Rainforest'
- White Sumatran tiger
- Platypus and echidna
- Views from the cable car
- Night zoo in October
- Discovery Park

INFORMATION

www.zoo.nsw.gov.au

➕ M3

✉ Bradleys Head Road, Mosman

☎ 9969 2777

🕐 Daily 9–5 (until 8 in Jan)

🍴 Variety of cafés and kiosks

🚌 247

🚢 Taronga Zoo

♿ Good

💲 Expensive

↔ Sydney Harbour (➤ 28), Mosman (➤ 57), Cremorne Point (➤ 60)

❓ Guided tours, special zoo-keeper presentations and talks

Located in Sydney Harbour, Taronga Zoo is a conservation leader. Although it doesn't limit itself to native animals, it's the Australian fauna most visitors come to see. The ferry ride to get there is a bonus.

Australian fauna Set in natural foreshore bushland, Taronga (an Aboriginal word meaning water view) dates from 1916 and has long been at the forefront of keeping animals in less restrictive enclosures. Arrive by ferry and take the Ski Safari up the zoo's steep incline to the top entrance. This is a great place to meet native Australian wildlife—you can see kangaroos, wallabies, dingoes, emus, wombats, the carnivorous Tasmanian devil, crocodiles and many striking birds. As always, the koalas are a must-see, particularly as you can have your photo taken next to one of these endearing creatures. Don't miss the spiky echidna and the aquatic platypus (examples of monotremes—strange, egg-laying mammals). Other highlights include Western Lowland gorillas, the very entertaining seal shows and the Discovery Park, which gives children (and adults) the opportunity to meet and even touch some of the feathered and furry residents. Taronga has a strong educational bias and a variety of animal presentations and keeper talks take place each day on anything from what koalas eat to the habits of giraffes. A night zoo operates throughout October.

Creatures from other countries Taronga's strong support for wildlife conservation is evident in its endangered species breeding agenda; the zoo is home to Sumatran tigers, Himalayan snow leopards, red pandas and orang-utans. You will also see more familiar zoo animals such as elephants, giraffes and chimpanzees.

National Maritime Museum

This comprehensive display of Australia's maritime heritage, from the arrival of the First Fleet to the modern voyages of Vietnamese boat people, documents Australia's inextricable links with the ocean.

Indoor displays Opened in 1991, the museum features seven themed sections—First People, Discovery, Commerce, Passengers, Leisure, Navy and Linked by the Sea—that contain thousands of items in displays as diverse as early beach fashions, the yacht *Australia II* (winner of the America's Cup in 1983) and migrant voyages. Other highlights include a section on Aboriginal people and the sea, the maritime links between Australia and the US and an intriguing display on how a Sydney man built the world's fastest boat in his back garden. You can also see what life was like on board a convict ship, discover why surfboards have become shorter, play with high-tech computer games or watch a film in the museum's cinema. As well as the thousands of exhibits in the permanent collection, temporary exhibitions are also presented regularly.

Outdoor displays Once you've seen what's on offer inside, go to the outdoor displays, moored at the museum's wharves. The 14 historic vessels include HMAS *Vampire*, the last of the Royal Australian Navy's big gunships, and one of the navy's submarines, both of which you can tour. Among the other interesting craft here are the *Arkarana*, an 1888 racing cutter, a Vietnamese refugee boat that reached northern Australia, a lugger from the pearling port of Broome in Western Australia and *Krait*, a World War II commando boat. From the wharves you can admire the building's unusual architecture.

HIGHLIGHTS

- HMAS *Vampire*
- Hands-on exhibits
- Vietnamese refugee boat
- Museum computer games
- America's Cup display
- Discovery section
- USA Gallery
- Navy submarine

INFORMATION

www.anmn.gov.au
- H6
- Darling Harbour West
- 9298 3777
- Daily 9.30–5; closed 25 Dec
- Good café
- Town Hall
- Sydney Explorer
- Monorail to Harbourside
- Aquarium Wharf
- Excellent
- Moderate
- Sydney Harbour (► 28), Sydney Aquarium and Darling Harbour (► 31, 62), Powerhouse Museum (► 36), Chinese Garden & Chinatown (► 40)
- Guided tours (included in admission price), films, maritime library, good shop

Chinese Garden & Chinatown

HIGHLIGHTS

- Garden's pavilions, lakes and waterfalls
- Sydney Entertainment Centre
- Paddy's Markets (➤ 70)
- Dixon Street
- Capitol Theatre (➤ 80)

INFORMATION

www.chinatownsydney.com

- ✚ J6–J7
- ✉ Chinese Garden: Darling Harbour
- ☎ 9281 0788
- ⏰ Daily 9.30–dusk
- 🍴 Cafés and restaurants nearby
- 🚉 Town Hall
- 🚌 Sydney Explorer
- 🚉 Monorail to Haymarket
- 🚢 Aquarium Wharf, Darling Harbour
- ♿ Good
- 💲 Inexpensive
- ↔ Sydney Aquarium & Darling Harbour (➤ 31, 62), Powerhouse Museum (➤ 36), National Maritime Museum (➤ 39)

The vibrant Chinese quarter, part of the city since the 1860s, is a great place for diverse Asian cuisines and speciality shopping. The Chinese Garden, just a few steps away from Chinatown, offers a calm retreat in the middle of busy downtown Sydney.

The Chinese Garden The largest of its kind outside mainland China, this tranquil garden was designed by Chinese landscape architects from Guangdong Province, a New South Wales sister state and features Cantonese-style pavilions, lakes, waterfalls and bridges. With its shrubs, flowers and trees, including maples, this is a delightful spot in which to relax after seeing Darling Harbour's myriad attractions. Its other name is the Garden of Friendship, symbolizing the enduring links between China and Australia. The garden offers a calm retreat from the hustle and bustle of the city. A tea house serves traditional Chinese tea and cakes and other refreshments.

Chinatown Centred on Dixon, Hay and Sussex streets, Sydney's Chinatown is a bustling area of Asian food and clothing shops, as well as many moderately-priced restaurants. Paddy's Markets are held here at weekends and the area includes the city's largest performance venue, the Sydney Entertainment Centre. The beautifully restored 1928 Capitol Theatre, home of major musical and theatrical events, is nearby on Campbell Street; it's worth seeing a show to appreciate the extraordinarily ornate interior. Chinese New Year (January or February) is a particularly exciting time to be in the area, when you will see fireworks, dragon dances and street processions.

Sydney Olympic Park

After hosting the 'best Olympics ever' Sydneysiders have taken the Games site to their hearts—you'll see them walking around with looks of awe. But you will find more than Olympic mem ories here as you can participate in a sport of your particular choice.

Learn about sport The massive facility built for the Sydney 2000 Olympic Games has been transformed into a focus site for entertainment and sport. The best way to get here is by RiverCat ferry from Circular Quay. Telstra Stadium, the site of the Olympic opening and closing ceremonies and focal point of Sydney Olympic Park, now hosts major rugby and football games. Guided tours run daily. The Sydney Showground, home to the annual Royal Easter Show, when the country comes to the city, also hosts sports events and rock concerts. The NSW Hall of Champions features photographs and memorabilia of athletes from the 1890s to the present. Sydney SuperDome, situated in the heart of Sydney Olympic Park, is the largest multi-use live entertainment and indoor sports arena in Australia.

Play sport Sydney Aquatic Centre has four world-class swimming pools. The complex also has spas, a sauna and steam room, a gym plus a children's water playground and a café. The Sydney International Tennis Centre has courts for rent and offers individual coaching. Sydney Indoor Sports Centre offers table tennis, badminton, volleyball, handball and netball.

Bicentenial Park 40ha (99 acres) of parklands set in an important wetland ecosystem. Facilities include free barbecues, picnic shelters, trails, play areas, bicycle paths and information point.

HIGHLIGHTS

- Sydney Aquatic Centre
- Telstra Stadium
- NSW Hall of Champions
- Bicentennial Park

INFORMATION

www.sydneyolymicpark.com.au

- off map to west
- Homebush Bay
- Park & Telstra Stadium 9714 7545
  NSW Hall of Champions & Sydney Showground 9763 0111
  Sydney SuperDome 8765 4321
  Bicentennial Park 9714 7300
- Park daily 24 hours
  Telstra Stadium daily 9.30–5.30
  NSW Hall of Champions daily 9–5
  Sydney SuperDome daily 8.30–5.30
  Bicentennial Park daily 6.30am–sunset
- Various
- Circular Quay/Central Station
- Circular Quay
- Excellent
- Park free; other attractions prices vary
- Guided tours available

41

Museum of Contemporary Art

HIGHLIGHTS

- Art-deco building
- Travelling exhibitions
- Indigenous art
- Works by Andy Warhol
- MCA shop and café

INFORMATION

www.mca.com.au

🔸 bi; J5

✉ Circular Quay West

☎ 9252 4033

🕐 Daily 10–5; closed Good Fri, 25 Dec

🍴 Café

🚉 Circular Quay

🚌 Sydney Explorer, 431, 432, 433

⛴ Circular Quay

♿ Excellent

🎟 Free

↔ Sydney Harbour Bridge (➤ 27), Sydney Harbour (➤ 28), Circular Quay (➤ 29), The Rocks (➤ 30), Sydney Observatory (➤ 50)

❓ Guided tours daily at 11 and 2, special films, talks and performances

The MCA is a modern art gallery full of surprises. Stunning installations, audacious photography, fine Aboriginal art and special performances all conjoin to astound and entertain.

The museum In a superb location overlooking the harbour, the MCA contains Australia's finest collection of contemporary art. Established in 1991 by the University of Sydney through a bequest of John Wardell Power and by the provision of the building by the state government, the MCA contains more than 4,000 works. International travelling exhibitions, ranging from photography to 3-D installations, are a highlight and often occupy most of the gallery space, sending much of the permanent collection into temporary storage.

The permanent collection The Australian and international art exhibits date from the 1960s and include indigenous art from the Northern Territory's Arnhem Land, the Contemporary Art Archive and work by overseas artists such as Andy Warhol and Roy Lichtenstein.

The building This old building was once home to the Maritime Services Board. The structure was designed in 1939 but was not completed until 1954 due to the war and shortages of building materials. This makes it the last art-deco style building in Sydney. The fine MCA Fish Café offers magnificent views of the Opera House.

Top: Exhibition of contemporary Australian art
Right: Circular Quay

Australian Museum

Rated among the world's top natural history museums, the Australian Museum highlights the country's unique fauna, geology and the history of Australia's Indigenous people.

The collection Housed in an 1849 building, with more recent additions, the museum has an excellent Aboriginal area, a showcase of native birds, insects and mammals and an informative display on gems and minerals. In other rooms you can discover more about human evolution, dinosaurs and Pacific and Indonesian peoples and their customs, including a traditional Indonesian gamelan orchestra, and try some enjoyable hands-on computer displays. One of the most interesting sections is the Skeletons room, where the internal organs of various creatures, including a cycling human, can be examined. And don't miss Eric, a 110- to 120-million-year-old plesiosaur; this opalized marine reptile was, incredibly, excavated far inland, at dusty Coober Pedy in South Australia.

Other highlights The excellent changing exhibitions here generally focus on environmental and cultural heritage topics. The College Street Diner has a lively atmosphere and the museum shop sells books on Australia, as well as unusual cards, gifts and souvenirs.

HIGHLIGHTS

- Aboriginal Australia display
- Planet of Minerals room
- Eric
- Australian birds, especially the parrots
- Human evolution displays
- Skeletons room

INFORMATION

www.amonline.net.au

- K6
- 6 College Street
- 9320 6000
- Daily 9.30–5; closed 25 Dec
- Two excellent cafés
- Museum
- Sydney Explorer, 311, 380, 382
- Very good
- Moderate. Free after 4pm
- Sydney Tower (➤ 33), Art Gallery of New South Wales (➤ 45), Anzac War Memorial (➤ 56), Hyde Park (➤ 62)
- Free tours daily; performances, special events and exhibitions; museum shop

Eric the plesiosaur

Royal Botanic Gardens & The Domain

HIGHLIGHTS

- Sydney Tropical Centre
- Sydney Fernery
- Palm Grove
- Visitor Centre and Gardens Shop
- Charlton Pool
- Government House (► 62)
- Walk around Farm Cove to Mrs Macquaries Point
- Views from Mrs Macquaries Point

INFORMATION

www.rbsyd.nsw.gov.au
- ci–cii; K5–K6
- Behind Farm Cove and off Mrs Macquaries Road
- Botanic Gardens 9231 8111. Government House infoline 9931 5222
- Gardens daily 8am–dusk. Glasshouses daily 10–4; closed Good Fri, 25 Dec. Government House Fri–Sun 10–3. Grounds daily 10–4
- Gardens restaurant/kiosk
- Circular Quay/Martin Place
- Sydney Explorer (to The Domain)
- Circular Quay
- Very good 🚻 Free
- Sydney Opera House (► 26), Sydney Harbour (► 28), Art Gallery of New South Wales (► 45), Hyde Park Barracks (► 47)
- Free guided walks, exhibitions

To escape the crowds of central Sydney, visit the glorious Botanic Gardens, once an Aboriginal sacred site, then take a stroll in the adjoining Domain, a harbourside haven for kookaburras, cockatoos and fruit bats.

Royal Botanic Gardens Extending inland from the curve of Farm Cove, these lovely gardens were the site of the first, rather unsuccessful, government farm back in 1788. The gardens were founded in 1816 and now contain a fine collection of native and foreign plants. The highlights include the lush Sydney Fernery and the Sydney Tropical Centre with its ultra-modern glasshouses. Here the wonders of tropical ecosystems are explained and there is a verdant display of plants from around the world. You can also wander through the delightful Palm Grove, or visit the beautifully laid-out Herb Garden, the Visitor Centre and Gardens Shop and the National Herbarium, established in 1985 to study Australia's native plants. The impressive Government House, once the official residence of the governor of NSW, lies within the gardens and is open to the public.

The Domain The northern section of The Domain (the remainder fronts the Art Gallery on the other side of the Cahill Expressway and is used mainly by lunchtime joggers and for open-air concerts in summer) is part of the land laid out in 1810 as the 'domain' of Governor Macquarie. This narrow, tree-lined area is a lovely spot for picnics and waterfront strolls. In summer, you can have a dip at the open-air Andrew 'Boy' Charlton swimming pool and walk to Mrs Macquaries Point, named after the governor's wife who, not surprisingly, enjoyed the wonderful view from this promontory.

Art Gallery of New South Wales

The Aboriginal material is a particularly exciting part of the wonderful collection of Australian, Asian and European art exhibited here. The local works of art offer a disparate view of Australian society and culture.

The collection The original Victorian building has been greatly extended (most recently to mark the 1988 bicentennial) to showcase the gallery's diverse permanent collection and the high-quality visiting international exhibitions. Besides work by European artists and fine Australian painters such as Frederick McCubbin, Arthur Streeton, Elioth Gruner, Lloyd Rees, Tom Roberts and Sidney Nolan, the gallery has an excellent Asian art section, whose ceramics are highly rated among connoisseurs. European highlights include works by Picasso, Van Gogh, Degas and Rodin, while the prints and drawings room and the photography gallery are also well worth visiting.

The Yiribana Gallery This newest exhibition is an exciting addition to the complex. It contains Australia's most comprehensive collection of Aboriginal and Torres Strait Islander art. More than 200 items, ranging from the most contemporary paintings to sculptures and traditional works on bark, are housed here. In addition, Aboriginal dance and music performances take place in the gallery at noon from Tuesday to Friday.

HIGHLIGHTS

- Yiribana Gallery
- Thai bronze Buddhas (Asian Art room)
- Elioth Gruner's Spring Frost
- Lloyd Rees's paintings
- Photography gallery
- Tom Roberts's paintings

INFORMATION

www.artgallery.nsw.gov.au
- ✚ ciii; K6
- ✉ Art Gallery Road, The Domain
- ☎ 9225 1744
- ⊘ Daily 10–5; closed Good Fri, 25 Dec
- 🍴 Excellent restaurant and café
- 🚇 St. James/Martin Place
- 🚌 Sydney Explorer
- ♿ Excellent
- 💲 Free
- ↔ City Centre (➤ 35), Royal Botanic Gardens & The Domain (➤ 44), Hyde Park Barracks (➤ 47)
- ❓ Free tours daily, lectures, films and performances; library and shop; Aboriginal dance and music

The Buddha enthroned under seven-headed naga (19th-century gilt bronze from the Thai, Bangkok period)

45

Museum of Sydney

HIGHLIGHTS

- *Edge of the Trees* sculpture and the public square
- Original Government House foundations
- Video wall
- Eora story
- Sydney environment displays

INFORMATION

www.hht.net.au

- ✛ bii; J5
- ✉ Corner of Bridge and Phillip streets
- ☎ 9251 5988
- ⏲ Daily 10–5; closed Good Fri, 25 Dec
- 🍴 Café
- 🚆 Circular Quay
- 🚌 Any Circular Quay-bound bus
- ⛴ Circular Quay
- ♿ Excellent
- ✋ Moderate
- ↔ Sydney Opera House (➤ 26), Circular Quay (➤ 29), Royal Botanic Gardens & The Domain (➤ 44)
- ❓ Guides available in the museum; exhibitions, lectures, performances; museum shop

This unusual museum leads you on an illuminating journey of discovery from the local Aboriginal occupation and the earliest convict days of the late 10th century to the emerging Sydney of the 1850s and beyond.

The site Where the museum is located forms an integral part of this exciting $29 million museum, opened in May 1995, for it was here the nation's first, modest Government House was built in 1788. Home to the first eight governors, the building was demolished in 1846, but excavations have revealed the original foundations, part of which can be viewed through the paving. Emphasizing the nation's mixed origins, the dramatic forecourt sculpture, *Edge of the Trees*, consists of 29 columns, remnants of Aboriginal and early European occupation.

The museum Divided into several themed areas and laid out in an imaginative minimalist style, the three-level Museum of Sydney aims to interpret the city's history from 1788 to 1850. Stories of the local Eora Aborigines and the early European days are told through artefacts found during the excavations, computer displays, an extraordinary 33-screen video wall and spoken history.

Top: Exhibits in the Museum of Sydney
Left: Edge of the Trees sculpture

Hyde Park Barracks

This building, once inhabited by convicts, was designed by the brilliant ex-forger turned architect Francis Greenway. Now a museum, the building has remarkable displays covering convict life and Sydney's early years.

The barracks Located on historic Macquarie Street, Hyde Park Barracks (1819) is perhaps the city's most charming building. Standing in dignified seclusion behind its grand gates, this three-floor example of Georgian architecture originally accommodated convicts and later became a home for destitute women. The building is now a fascinating museum, focusing on the lives of these occupants and providing a glimpse into Sydney's early days. Changing exhibitions are mounted on the ground-floor Greenway Gallery. The most enjoyable way to appreciate the simple but elegant building, however, is by taking a coffee or meal at the delightful Hyde Park Barracks Café situated in the courtyard.

Queens Square and Macquarie Street The city's finest and most historically significant avenue, Macquarie Street, begins outside the barracks at Queens Square, which is anchored by an 1888 statue of Queen Victoria. This area contains the city's oldest church, the 1822 St. James (another Francis Greenway building), the modern Law Courts and other historic structures such as the 1816 Sydney Mint. To appreciate thoroughly Macquarie Street's charms, walk past Victorian Sydney Hospital, the Sydney Mint and State Parliament House (1816) to the State Library. Beyond Bent Street you can view the 1819 Conservatorium of Music, also designed by Francis Greenway, which adjoins the Royal Botanic Gardens.

HIGHLIGHTS

- Elegant architecture
- Exhibitions in the Greenway Gallery
- Historic Macquarie Street
- St. James Church
- Statue of Queen Victoria

INFORMATION

- www.hht.net.au
- ciii; K6
- Queens Square, Macquarie Street
- 9223 8922
- Daily 10–5; closed Good Fri, 25 Dec
- Hyde Park Barracks Café (➤ 70)
- Martin Place/St. James
- Sydney Explorer, 311
- Circular Quay
- Few
- Moderate
- Sydney Tower (➤ 33), Royal Botanic Gardens & The Domain (➤ 44), Art Gallery of New South Wales (➤ 45), Museum of Sydney (➤ 46)
- Guided tours, exhibitions, special tours and events

Sydney Observatory

HIGHLIGHTS

- Night-sky viewing
- Hands-on scientific exhibits
- View from Observatory Hill
- S.H. Ervin Gallery
- Argyle Place
- Garrison Church
- Having a beer in the Lord Nelson Hotel (➤ 82)

INFORMATION

www.powerhousemuseum.com
✚ ai; J4
✉ Observatory Hill, Millers Point
☎ 9217 0485
🕐 Daily 10–5 (late opening evenings according to season, telephone for details). Closed Good Fri, 25 Dec
🍴 Café nearby
🚊 Circular Quay
🚌 431, 432, 433
🚢 Circular Quay
♿ Few
💵 Free; charge for night viewing
🔄 Sydney Harbour Bridge (➤ 27), Circular Quay (➤ 29), The Rocks (➤ 30)
❓ Guided tours, night viewing, talks, exhibitions and films

View from the rotunda in Observatory Park along out into the harbour

Sydney's glittering night skies, so different from those in the northern hemisphere, are as intriguing now as they were for Australia's early astronomers, who erected this fine building high on Observatory Hill in 1858.

The Observatory and Observatory Hill The Observatory, now a museum of astronomy and related sciences, provides a fascinating glimpse into those studies through entertaining hands-on exhibits and other displays. This is also the location for one of Sydney's most unusual tourist activities—night-sky viewing, which must be reserved in advance. Observatory Hill is the city centre's highest point (44m/119ft) and was the site of Fort Phillip (1803), the original 1821 Observatory and the Signal Station (1848), which still stands today. There are great inner-harbour views from the hill and you can walk behind the Observatory to visit the National Trust Centre, with its S.H. Ervin Gallery and excellent tearooms. The gallery features changing exhibitions of Australian art and culture, ranging from watercolour paintings to photography.

Argyle Place Just below Observatory Hill and flanked by historic houses and the 1840 Gothic-revival Garrison Church is Argyle Place, the city's only village green. Also here is the sandstone Lord Nelson Hotel (1834), licensed since 1842 and Sydney's oldest watering hole. A stroll down nearby Lower Fort Street reveals more 19th-century terraced houses and the charming, oddly shaped Hero of Waterloo Hotel (1844), the city's second-oldest pub. From just above Argyle Place, you can walk, via the covered steps, on to the Sydney Harbour Bridge walkway.

SYDNEY's
best

51

The Great Outdoors

ADVENTURE ACTIVITIES

Few cities in the world can offer outdoor adventures just minutes from the heart of the city. In Sydney you can hike, dive, windsurf or sail, or even go rappeling on various cliffs. Details of operators are available from www.letstrekaustralia.com

CREMORNE POINT RESERVE

This walk reveals a portion of the city that visitors seldom see, and lies just a short ferry ride from Circular Quay. From the wharf, turn left and walk along the reserve's western section, which gives fine views of the city. By walking up the steps opposite the wharf and heading to the left, you can stroll around the harbourside, past lush gardens and homes with superb outlooks, to tranquil Mosman Bay. From here, the ferry will take you to Circular Quay.

🚉 L3 ✉ Cremorne ⏰ Daily ⛴ Cremorne Point 🎟 Free

LADY BAY BEACH

For some, the ultimate in getting back to nature involves stripping off and spending the day at a nudist beach. This idyllic harbourside area is one of Sydney's most popular *au naturel* spots, and lies just a short walk from Camp Cove at Watsons Bay.

🚉 Off map to east ✉ Watsons Bay ⏰ Daily 🍴 At Watsons Bay
🚌 324, 325 (or ferry to Watsons Bay) 🎟 Free

Sunbathers and motorboats at Manly Cove

NORTH HEAD

The impressive national park-protected outcrop of North Head looms above Manly and the harbour, with incredible views from its various lookouts.

⊞ Off map to northeast ☎ 9247 5033 🕐 Daily 🍴 In Manly 🚢 Manly 💰 Free

NORTHERN NATIONAL PARKS

The greater Sydney region contains no less than 10 national parks, as well as many other natural reserves. In the north you can visit Cattai, Lane Cove, Garigal and magnificent Ku-ring-gai Chase, although you need to have your own vehicle or take a tour to fully appreciate these superb wilderness areas.

⊞ Off map to north ☎ 9457 9322 🕐 Daily 🍴 Kiosks and picnic areas 💰 Inexpensive

SOUTHERN NATIONAL PARKS

The city's southern national parks—Botany Bay and the Royal, Georges River, Thirlmere Lakes and Heathcote—offer scenery ranging from freshwater lakes to spectacular beaches. Your own transport is necessary, or contact Allambie Mini Buses.

⊞ Off map to south ☎ 9542 0666 for group reservations 🕐 Daily 🍴 Kiosks and picnic areas 💰 Inexpensive

THE SPIT TO MANLY WALK

This 8-km (5-mile) harbourside walk takes three to four hours and passes through undeveloped bushland and the waterfront suburbs surrounding Manly; views of the harbour and city are magnificent. Further information is available from the National Parks Service.

⊞ Off map to north ✉ From the Spit Bridge, Middle Harbour ☎ National Parks Service 9247 5033 🕐 Daily 🍴 At Manly 🚌 178, 180, 182, 190 💰 Free

SYDNEY HARBOUR NATIONAL PARK

Designated in 1975, Sydney Harbour National Park encompasses islands and pockets of remarkably unspoiled bushland around the harbour. There are many beaches to enjoy, walks in the bush, historic sites and even Aboriginal carvings.

⊞ N2–N4 ☎ 9247 5033 🕐 Daily 🍴 Kiosks and picnic areas 💰 Free

WATSONS BAY AND SOUTH HEAD

In the early 1800s Watsons Bay was a fishing hamlet and military base. Today, this charming suburb has retained its village atmosphere. There are great views of the harbour, swimming at Camp Cove and an enjoyable walk to South Head National Park.

⊞ Off map to east ☎ 9337 5511 🕐 Daily 🍴 Cafés and restaurants 🚌 324, 325 🚢 Watsons Bay 💰 Free

---

SYDNEY'S BEACHES

Sydney's great outdoors is epitomized by the many beaches dotted along its harbour and extensive coastline. Popular harbour beaches are Nielsen Park (► 49) and northside Balmoral. Other than Bondi and Manly, good surf beaches include Coogee, Maroubra and Cronulla to the south and the wonderful northern beaches that stretch from Manly to Palm Beach.

LEARN TO SURF

Waves Surf School (☎ 1800 851 101) runs 1, 2 and 4-day surf trips to top surf locations. All standards are catered for.

Galleries & Museums

MUSEUMS IN THE ROCKS

The Rocks contains several small but interesting museums. The best are the Merchants' House (✉ 43 George Street), featuring a collection of rare children's books and toys; Susannah Place (✉ 58–64 Gloucester Street), an entire terrace of four restored houses; and the Westpac Museum (✉ 6–8 Playfair Street), which tells the story of Australian banking.

AUSTRALIAN CENTRE FOR PHOTOGRAPHY

Australia's premier photography gallery, established in 1973, has two exhibition spaces, a project wall for emerging artists, a workshop with public access and a specialist bookshop. For practioners there is a darkroom facility, a digital workstation and a research library. The gallery is a non-profit making organization.
➕ L8 ✉ 257 Oxford Street, Paddington ☎ 9332 1455
🕐 Tue–Sun 11–6 🍴 Nearby 🚌 378, 380, 382 ✋ Free

BRETT WHITELEY STUDIO

This museum and gallery, opened in 1995, is a tribute to Brett Whiteley, born in 1939, one of Australia's most important and controversial modern artists, who died of a drug overdose in 1993. His studio, now refurbished by the NSW government, is full of his sculptures, paintings, drawings and memorabilia.
➕ K8 ✉ 2 Raper Street, Surry Hills ☎ 9225 1881 🕐 Sat–Sun 10–4 🍴 Nearby 🚌 302, 372 ✋ Moderate

HARRIS STREET MOTOR MUSEUM

Located not far from the Powerhouse (➤ 36), this intriguing museum is dedicated to the display of around 200 classic motor cars, commercial vehicles and bikes, and tells the story of the automotive industry over the past century or so.
➕ H6 ✉ 320 Harris Street (corner of Allen Street), Pyrmont ☎ 9252 4033 🕐 Daily 11–6 🍴 Nearby 🚃 Monorail to Convention Centre ✋ Moderate

JUSTICE AND POLICE MUSEUM

Originally the Water Police Court (1856), these atmospheric old buildings now house a museum of legal and police history. The complex includes the Magistrate's Court, exhibitions in the cells and a museum of crime, the latter featuring mug shots of some of early Sydney's criminals.
➕ cii; K5 ✉ 8 Phillip Street ☎ 9252 1144 🕐 Sat–Sun 10–5 (also Sat–Thu in Jan) 🍴 Nearby 🚉 Circular Quay ✋ Moderate

MARY MACKILLOP MUSEUM

Beatified in 1995, Mary MacKillop was a determined leader who made a huge contribution to the status of the poor in Australia. State-of-the-art electronics,

The Justice and Police Museum

animatronics and powerful theatrics show Mary's life and how in 1866, at the age of 24, she opened her first Josephite school and founded an institute for women. Also found at this museum is Mary MacKillop's tomb and memorial chapel, Alma Cottage, where she lived and, in 1909, died.

🚩 J2 ✉ Mary MacKillop Place, 7 Mount Street, North Sydney ☎ 8912 4878 🕐 Daily 10–4; closed 25 Dec 🍴 Coffee shop 🚉 North Sydney 💷 Moderate

QUARANTINE STATION

Used since the 1830s to protect Sydney from smallpox, bubonic plague and other contagious diseases by quarantining migrants, the station is now an unusual museum. You can see the burial grounds, rock engravings and various displays, while night-time ghost tours of the reputedly haunted complex, complete with tales of strange happenings, are a spooky alternative.

🚩 Off map to northeast ✉ North Head, Manly ☎ 9977 6732 🕐 Tours daily 1.10pm 🚢 Manly, then bus 135 💷 Moderate

SYDNEY JEWISH MUSEUM

The ground floor of this museum is devoted to Australian Jewish history and documenting the gradual development of a community. Other intriguing displays explain special festivals and customs and provide a glimpse into the Jewish religion and the traditional emphasis on family values. Upstairs is a memorial to the six million Jews who perished in the Holocaust. The museum also hosts temporary exhibitions and organizes lectures.

🚩 J4 ✉ Corner of Darlinghurst Road and Burton Street, Darlinghurst ☎ 9331 4245 🕐 Sun–Thu 10–4, Fri 10–2 🍴 Nearby 🚌 311, 389 💷 Moderate

COMMERCIAL ART GALLERIES

If you are interested in exploring the modern Australian art scene, pay a visit to some of Sydney's commercial galleries, including Hogarth Galleries Aboriginal Art (✉ 7 Walker Lane, Paddington); Wagner Art Gallery (✉ 39 Gurner Street, Paddington); and the Roslyn Oxley Gallery (✉ Soudan Lane, off 27 Hampden Street, Paddington).

Architecture & Interiors

WALKING TOURS

If you are interested in Sydney's historic areas and architecture, join a guided walking tour. Such tours operate in The Rocks (➤ 30), while Sydney Guided Tours (☎ 9660 7157) can take you on informative strolls to places such as historic churches, the suburb of Balmain and Sydney University.

ANZAC WAR MEMORIAL

This huge 1934 art-deco structure, decorated with poignant sculptures, is Sydney's tribute to those who died during World War I. Inside, the domed ceiling is covered with stars representing World War I volunteers, while the lower level features a photographic exhibition.

✚ J6 ✉ Hyde Park South ⏰ Mon–Sat 10–4, Sun 1–4; closed Good Fri and 25 Dec 🍴 Nearby 🚇 Museum 🎫 Free

CHIFLEY TOWER

Nearly all of Sydney's newer skyscrapers have interesting rooflines. Chifley Tower, built in 1993, is one of them and also has some very chic shops and marble and terrazzo walkways inside.

✚ biii; J5 ✉ Chifley Square ☎ 9221 4500 ⏰ Daily 🍴 Cafés and restaurants 🚇 Martin Place 🎫 Free

ELIZABETH BAY HOUSE

Constructed from Sydney sandstone, the simple but elegant Elizabeth Bay House was built between 1835 and 1839. The house's most important feature is its oval-shaped saloon and winding staircase, regarded as Australia's finest. Rooms are open to the public and are furnished in Regency style.

✚ ciii; L6 ✉ 7 Onslow Avenue, Elizabeth Bay ☎ 9356 3022 ⏰ Tue–Sun 10–4.30 🍴 Nearby 🚇 Kings Cross 🎫 Moderate

*Victoria Barracks'
impressive sandstone
façade*

PADDINGTON HOUSES

Paddington's terraced (row) houses, with their iron lacework fences and balconies, are delightful. Built between the 1860s and1890s as housing for workers, most have been restored to create a charming suburb, listed as a conservation area by the National Trust.

📍 L7–M7　✉　► 17　🍴 Nearby　🚌 378, 380, 382　💵 Free

ROSE SEIDLER HOUSE

Completed in 1950, this uncomprisingly modernist house was designed by Australia's leading architect, Harry Seidler. Features include glass walls, open-plan living areas and a minimal colour scheme. Its original furniture comprises one of the most important post-war design collections in Australia. You will have to visit by car as there is no public transport.

📍 Off map to north　✉ 71 Clissold Road, Wahroonga　☎ 9989 8020
🕐 Sun 10–5　💵 Inexpensive

STATE PARLIAMENT HOUSE

Originally part of the Rum Hospital, Parliament House (built in 1816), with its shady verandas, is a fine example of early colonial architecture. You can take a tour of the building, but it is advisable to make a reservation.

📍 ciii; K5　✉ Macquarie Street　☎ Tours 9230 2047　🕐 Tours Mon–Fri 9–5　🍴 Nearby　🚇 Martin Place　💵 Free

VICTORIA BARRACKS

This imposing National Trust-listed 1840s building was constructed by soldiers and convicts and boasts a 226-m (610-ft) long sandstone façade. Guided tours include a band performance, the military museum and other sections of the historic base, which is still occupied by the Australian Army.

📍 L7　✉ Oxford Street, Paddington　☎ 9339 3330　🕐 Tours Thu 10am. Museum Sun 10–3　🍴 Nearby　🚌 378, 380, 382　💵 Free

Exquisite lacework balconies in Paddington

MOSMAN

Mosman, with magnificent harbour views, is one of Sydney's most affluent suburbs. It lies on the northern side of the Harbour Bridge, just a few minutes by ferry from Circular Quay. Architecturally, the homes are a mix of late 19th-century mansions, California- and Federation-style homes and modern apartments. Military Road, the suburb's main thoroughfare, is the preserve of designer-clothing boutiques, antiques galleries, fine food shops and cafés. Nearby Balmoral has one of the harbour's prettiest beaches, a number of waterfront restaurants and a first-class fish shop, so good that people line up for its excellent seafood.

Other Attractions

AUSTRALIAN WILDLIFE

Australia's unique wildlife is irresistible and the wildlife parks and zoos detailed here offer the chance to cuddle koalas, meet kangaroos and other marsupials and see a variety of incredibly vivid birds. You will also be able to observe the strange egg-laying monotremes, the platypus and echidna. A word of advice: The easiest way to reach most of these suburban parks is on an organized tour (➤ 20).

KATOOMBA SCENIC SKYWAY & RAILWAY

Rides on either the Scenic Skyway, which straddles precipitous Jamieson Valley, or the fast-plunging Scenic Railway combine heart-in-the-mouth thrills and glorious bushland vistas to keep everyone in the family happy.

✚ Off map to west ✉ Corner of Cliff Drive and Violet Street, Katoomba, Blue Mountains ☎ 4782 2699 ◉ Daily ❙❙ Restaurant, picnic/barbecue areas nearby ◩ Katoomba ◧ Inexpensive

KOALA PARK SANCTUARY

In this famous private koala sanctuary, in operation since 1930, you can cuddle koalas, hand-feed kangaroos and see traditional bush activities such as sheep shearing and boomerang throwing. Check out th birds too, including wedge-tailed eagles and rainbow lorikeets.

✚ Off map to northwest ✉ 84 Castle Hill Road, West Pennant Hills ☎ 9484 3141 ◉ Daily 9–5; closed 25 Dec ❙❙ Kiosk and picnic/ barbecue area ◩ Pennant Hills, then buses 651–5 ◧ Expensive

LUNA PARK

This superbly restored 1930s amusement park, with some of the best city views, offers rides, entertainment under the big top, and a range of food and beverage outlets.

✚ J3 ✉ Olympic Drive, Milsons Point ☎ 9922 6646 ◉ Daily 10–10 ❙❙ Cafés, bars and restaurant ◩ Milson Point or take ferry ◧ Free entry

STAR CITY SYDNEY

Gamblers are encouraged to try their luck at games such as blackjack, roulette, poker and pai gow. There are also 1,500 slot machines, cafés and restaurants and the 2,000-seat Lyric Theatre, which hosts acts by international entertainers.

✚ H5 ✉ 80 Pyrmont Street, Pyrmont ☎ 9777 9000 ◉ Daily 24 hours ❙❙ Numerous restaurants and cafés ◩ Star City Light Rail ◧ Free entry

SYDNEY HARBOUR CRUISES

Unwind on a fine day and learn about the harbour, its bays and waterways on a variety of cruises. Depart from Circular Quay (➤ 29).

✚ J5 ✉ Captain Cook Cruises, No. 6 Jetty, Circular Quay NSW 2000 ☎ 9206 1122 ◉ Daily from 9.30am ❙❙ Coffee and dinner cruises ◩ Circular Quay ◧ Moderate

TALL SHIP *JAMES CRAIG*

One of the only four working 19th-century tall ships in the world, now taking passengers on sailing adventures off Sydney Heads on alternate weekends. Join the crew hoisting the sails or just enjoy the views.

✚ J4 ☎ 9298 3888; www.austfleet.com ⊕ Alternate weekends 🍴 Sailor's boxed lunch ✋ Moderate

WARATAH PARK EARTH SANCTUARY

Waratah Park, the closest wildlife park to the city, features koalas, emus, birds, kangaroos and other native fauna. The bushland setting can be appreciated from the short Bush Railroad ride.

✚ Off map to north 🚗 Namba Road, Duffy's Forest ☎ 9886 1788 ⊕ Daily 4pm–9pm; closed 25 Dec 🍴 Snack bar and barbecues 🚌 Chatswood, then a special bus service ✋ Moderate

BEACHES FOR KIDS

Most of Sydney's surf beaches are not suitable for younger children, so if you are visiting in summer, head for sheltered spots such as Camp Cove at Watsons Bay, Nielsen Park (Vaucluse) and, north of the harbour, Balmoral or Shelly Beach at Manly. Bronte, although a surf beach, also has an ocean pool, a large park and a good playground area for children.

The koala is a marsupial, not a bear

Views

THE BEST VIEWS IN TOWN

To appreciate Sydney's spectacular harbour, the city skyline and the Opera House from a great perspective, the three-hour BridgeClimb makes for an unusual tour of Harbour Bridge. Professional guides accompany you on day and night climbs. Reservations (☎ 8274 7777) are essential. Red Baron Scenic Flights (☎ 9791 0044), operating out of Rose Bay, include aerobatics over the harbour in their open-cockpit biplane.

Rushcutters Bay, near Kings Cross

CREMORNE POINT

Take a ferry ride to the north shore and enjoy the views of Sydney Harbour and the city skyline. Walk to Robertsons Point, or to Cremorne Point Reserve (► 52) and MacCallum Pool.

➕ L3 ✉ Cremorne 🚢 Cremorne Point 🖐 Free

HORIZON COCKTAIL BAR

This aptly named cocktail bar, on the 36th floor of the Shangri-la Hotel, has fantastic views.

➕ aii; J5 ✉ Shangri-la Hotel Sydney, 176 Cumberland Street, The Rocks ☎ 9250 6000 🍴 Restaurants in hotel 🚊 Circular Quay 🖐 The cost of a drink

MACKENZIES POINT

This promontory gives you wonderful views of the beach at Bondi, out to the Pacific Ocean and south down the rugged coast.

➕ Off map to east ✉ South of Bondi Beach 🚌 380, 382 🖐 Free

MCKELL PARK

This pleasant reserve is great for picnics and for admiring the harbour. You can explore Darling Point and continue to Rushcutters Bay and its marina.

➕ M5 ✉ Darling Point Road, Darling Point 🕐 Daily during daylight hours 🚢 Darling Point 🖐 Free

NEW SOUTH HEAD ROAD, ROSE BAY

The hill north of Rose Bay offers one of the best harbour panoramas in Sydney.

➕ Off map to east ✉ Near the junction with Vaucluse Road 🚌 324, 325 🖐 Free

Interesting Suburbs

GLEBE

Glebe offers offbeat shopping, a Saturday market and good-value restaurants, while the University of Sydney (established in 1850 and Australia's oldest university) features grand buildings and the superb Nicholson Museum with its famous archaeological collection.

🔲 G7, G8 ☎ Museum 9351 2812 🏛 Museum Mon–Fri 10–4.30; closed 25 Dec–Jan 🍴 Many cafés and restaurants 🚌 431 💲 Free

HUNTERS HILL

An attractive suburb worth visiting for the ferry ride west of the Harbour Bridge and for a look at 1871 Vienna Cottage. This fine example of a small stone tradesman's house also has a small museum. Hunters Hill is a designated conservation area, so sample its refined atmosphere on the walk from the wharf.

🔲 D2 ✉ Vienna Cottage, 38 Alexandra Street ☎ 9817 2510 🏛 Museum: 2nd & 4th Sun 2–4 ⛴ Valentia Street 💲 Free. Vienna Cottage inexpensive

KINGS CROSS AND POTTS POINT

Once Sydney's most Bohemian district, Kings Cross is now rather seedy, but it's still interesting and *the* place for late nightlife. Potts Point (Macleay and Victoria streets in particular) is full of cafés and old houses.

🔲 L6 🍴 Many cafés and restaurants 🚇 Kings Cross 💲 Free

WOOLLOOMOOLOO

This inner-city address, with its extraordinary Aboriginal name, offers quaint terraced (row) houses and a few other attractions. On Cowper Wharf Road you will find the historic Finger Wharf that juts far out into the bay, ships of the Australian Navy's fleet and Artspace, a gallery of contemporary art.

🔲 diii; K6 ✉ Artspace, 43–51 Cowper Wharf Road ☎ 9368 1899 🏛 Mon–Sat 11–6; closed hols 🍴 Nearby 🚌 311 💲 Free

HARBOURSIDE SUBURBS

Waterfront suburbs that are great for walks and picnics are Darling Point, Rose Bay, historic Watsons Bay (➤ 53) and Cremorne on the north side (➤ 60), all reached by ferry from Circular Quay. You can also shop until you drop at north shore Mosman (➤ 57) and at Double Bay in the eastern suburbs.

Hunters Hill, an expensive and fashionable Sydney suburb

What's Free

GOVERNMENT HOUSE

Built between 1837 and 1845, Government House at the lower end of Macquarie Street, is considered the most sophisticated example of a Gothic Revival building in the state. The state rooms display a vast array of period designs and furnishings.
☎ Infoline 9931 5222
⊙ Fri–Sun 10–3; grounds daily 10–4

DARLING HARBOUR

As well as offering major attractions such as Sydney Aquarium and the National Maritime Museum, Darling Harbour is great for free music and other entertainment, particularly around the Harbourside shopping complex or in Tumbalong Park.
✚ H6–J6 ☎ 9281 0788 ❚❚ Many cafés and restaurants
◼ Monorail to Harbourside ◗ Free

HYDE PARK

This CBD haven has been a park since 1810 and is a popular lunchtime spot for city workers. You can wander among formal gardens and tree-lined paths and visit the Anzac War Memorial (► 56).
✚ biv–civ; J6 ✉ Off Elizabeth Street ⊙ Daily ❚❚ Nearby
◼ St. James ◗ Free

MARTIN PLACE

Martin Place, the city's largest pedestrian area, offers free entertainment during weekday lunchtimes—try the amphitheatre near Castlereagh Street.
✚ biii; J5 ✉ Between Macquarie and George streets ❚❚ Several cafés ◼ Martin Place ◗ Free

STATE LIBRARY OF NEW SOUTH WALES

More than just a library, this large complex has a good shop, free films, exhibitions (a small charge for some) and tours. You can also browse among the vast collection of books and other material on Australia.
✚ ciii; K5 ✉ Macquarie Street ☎ 9273 1414 ⊙ Mon–Fri 9–9, Sat–Sun 11–5; closed 1 Jan, Good Fri, Easter Sun, 25–26 Dec
❚❚ Licensed café ◼ Martin Place ◗ Free

SYDNEY OPEN MUSEUM

The many statues, fountains and outdoor monuments under the care of Sydney City Council have been declared the 'Sydney Open Museum'—a free attraction that provides you with a good excuse to wander the streets. Starting from Hyde Park, the trail takes you to Circular Quay and The Rocks before returning to central Sydney. An informative leaflet and map are available from the council's One-Stop Shop on the corner of Kent and Druitt streets.
✚ J6–J4 ✉ Start in Hyde Park South ☎ 1300 651 301
⊙ Mon–Fri ❚❚ Many cafés en route ◼ St. James/Museum ◗ Free

Darling Harbour has some of Sydney's most stimulating new buildings

SYDNEY
where to...

Modern Australian Restaurants

PRICES

The following price guide for restaurants is shown in Australian dollars. Expect to pay per person, excluding drinks and tips:

$ up to $30
$$ $30–$50
$$$ more than $50

EATING OUT IN SYDNEY

Sydney restaurants range from super-inexpensive to the totally indulgent, while cuisines from all over the world are represented. Australian wines are a wonderful accompaniment to meals and a large proportion of restaurants are BYO (bring your own alcohol)—a small corkage fee is usually charged. Reserving is generally recommended, but many brasserie-style establishments do not accept reservations. Smoking is banned in all cafés and restaurants and in the dining section of pubs and clubs.

BATHERS PAVILION RESTAURANT ($$$)

Lush interior with views over the beach. Offers Mediterranean-style and classic Asian dishes.
✚ N1 ✉ 4 The Esplanade, Balmoral Beach ☎ 9969 5050 ⏰ Daily lunch, dinner

BILLS ($)

A popular breakfast and lunch spot for those on the run.
✚ K7 ✉ 433 Liverpool Street, Darlinghurst ☎ 9360 4762 ⏰ Daily breakfast, lunch 🚇 Museum

BISTRO MONCUR ($$–$$$)

Highly rated, innovative food in a trendy eastern suburbs pub. A bit noisy.
✚ M8 ✉ Woollahra Hotel, 116 Queen Street, Woollahra ☎ 9363 2519 ⏰ Thu–Sun lunch, daily dinner 🚌 389

CAFE SYDNEY ($$)

Great location overlooking Circular Quay, a lively cocktail bar serving innovative Australian food. Live jazz on Friday nights.
✚ bii; J5 ✉ Level 5, Customs House, Alfred Street ☎ 9251 8683 ⏰ Daily lunch, Mon–Sat dinner 🚉 Circular Quay

CARGO BAR ($$)

One of the best of the many King Street Wharf eateries. Enjoy pasta and pizzas alfresco.
✚ aiii; J6 ✉ 52 The Promenade, King Street Wharf ☎ 9262 1777 ⏰ Daily lunch, dinner 🚉 Darling Harbour

CATALINA ($$$)

One of Sydney's best; diners come here to be seen and to relish the Japanese-inspired dishes with a touch of Mediterranean influence. The sushi is a specialty.
✚ Off map to east ✉ Lyne Park, Rose Bay ☎ 9371 0555 ⏰ Daily lunch, dinner 🚌 324, 325

CIVIC DINING ($)

This classic art deco pub features a hip cocktail bar and a range of Asian/Oz dishes and tasty desserts.
✚ J7 ✉ Corner Pitt and Goulburn streets ☎ 8080 7040 ⏰ Tue–Fri lunch, Tue–Sat dinner 🚉 Town Hall

EDNA'S TABLE ($$–$$$)

Striking decor and the use of indigenous herbs and oils are highlights here. Your chance to try kangaroo, emu, crocodile or buffalo.
✚ G7 ✉ 204 Clarence Street, ☎ 9267 3933 ⏰ Mon–Fri lunch, Mon–Sat dinner 🚉 Town Hall

FORTY ONE ($$$)

Panoramic views and inventive cuisine make this one of the hottest dining spots in town. Reserve ahead.
✚ biii; J5 ✉ Level 41, Chifley Tower, Chifley Square ☎ 9221 2500 ⏰ Mon–Fri lunch, Mon–Sat dinner 🚉 Martin Place

GALILEO ($$$)

This traditional restaurant offers a variety of Italian-influenced dishes and a top-of-the-range wine menu.
✚ biii; J5 ✉ Observatory Hotel, 89–113 Kent Street ☎ 9256 2215 ⏰ Mon–Fri lunch, daily dinner 🚉 Circular Quay

HARBOUR KITCHEN & BAR ($$)

Part of the Park Hyatt, and offering fine harbour views, this hotel restaurant serves light meals and a full à la carte including twice-cooked duck breast with roasted peaches.

➕ J4 ✉ Park Hyatt Hotel, 7 Hickson Road ☎ 9256 1661 🕓 Daily lunch, dinner 🚌 431

MG GARAGE ($$$)

Amazingly, this place doubles as a car showroom. Come here for the fine seafood and exotic dishes presented with great style.

➕ K7 ✉ 490 Crown Street, Surry Hills ☎ 9383 9388 🕓 Mon–Fri lunch, Mon–Sat dinner 🚌 380, 390

PAVILION ON THE PARK ($$$)

Enjoy lunch on the terrace with quintessential Sydney vistas. Popular for its good selection of seafood dishes but try the roast lamb loin.

➕ ciii; K6 ✉ 1 Art Gallery Road, The Domain ☎ 9232 1322 🕓 Sun–Fri lunch 🚊 St. James/Martin Place

QUADRANT ($$$)

Great Circular Quay views. Plenty of seafood dishes; try crab tortellini or the ocean trout on saffron taglierini.

➕ cii; K5 ✉ Quay Grand Suites, 61–69 Macquarie Street ☎ 9256 4000 🕓 Mon–Fri breakfast, lunch and dinner, Sat dinner 🚊 Circular Quay

QUAY ($$$)

Seafood is a specialty here. Wonderful views of the Opera House and harbour.

➕ bi; J4 ✉ Upper level, Overseas Passenger Terminal Circular Quay West ☎ 9251 5600 🕓 Mon–Fri lunch, daily dinner 🚊 Circular Quay

SALT ($$$)

One of Sydney's hippest eating places. The food is original and classy with good vegetarian options.

➕ K7 ✉ Kirketon Hotel, 229 Darlinghurst Road, Darlinghurst ☎ 9332 2566 🕓 Mon–Fri lunch, daily dinner 🚌 380 (then walk down Darlinghurst Road)

SEAN'S PANORAMA ($$$)

Expect fresh seasonal produce transformed into innovative Med/Oz cuisine. The lovely sea views, attentive staff and good wine list are a bonus.

➕ Off map to east ✉ 270 Campbell Parade, Bondi ☎ 9365 4924 🕓 Sat, Sun lunch, Wed–Sat dinner 🚌 380, 382

TETSUYA'S ($$$)

Japanese cuisine transformed to an Australian art form by one of Sydney's top chefs.

➕ J6 ✉ 529 Kent Street ☎ 9267 2900 🕓 Fri–Sat lunch, Tue–Sat dinner 🚊 Town Hall 🚌 438

WATERMARK ($$$)

A comfortable cab ride from central Sydney to possibly the harbour's most beautiful venue.

➕ N1 ✉ 2a The Esplanade, Balmoral Beach ☎ 9968 3433 🕓 Daily lunch, dinner 🚢 Taronga Zoo Wharf, then bus 238

MODERN AUSTRALIAN CUISINE

Not so long ago, Australian cooking revolved around meat and three soggy vegetables, plus 'sophisticated' dishes like shrimp cocktail and stroganoff. An exciting new Australian cuisine has emerged, however, influenced by the eating habits of migrant Italians, Thais, Chinese and others. This experimental cooking might blend French and Thai styles, or local fish with Lebanese ingredients, to create a great dining experience. Bush tucker—such as kangaroo, crocodile and native plants—is another interesting addition to the Sydney restaurant scene.

Seafood Restaurants

AUSTRALIAN SEAFOOD

It is not surprising that seafood is so popular in this oceanside city. Local specialties include Sydney rock oysters, while kingfish, enormous shrimps, Tasmanian scallops and smoked salmon, South Australian tuna and northern fish such as the delicious barramundi grace menus all over town. Appropriately, many seafood restaurants have waterfront locations and you can also enjoy excellent take-out fish-and-chips—Bondi, Balmoral and Manly are particularly good spots for such alfresco eating.

BALKAN SEAFOOD ($$)

Chargrilled octopus, calamari and fish. BYO.
✚ K7 ✉ 215 Oxford Street, Darlinghurst ☎ 9331 7670
🕐 Tue–Sun dinner 🚍 380

BUNGALOW ($$)

Start at the upstairs Left Bar and work up an appetite for the fresh seafood dishes that include prawn (shrimp) specialties.
✚ J6 ✉ 8 The Promenade, King Street Wharf, Darling Harbour ☎ 9299 4660
🕐 Daily lunch, dinner
🚇 Town Hall

DOYLES ON THE BEACH ($$–$$$)

Sydney's most famous seafood restaurant, with great food and wonderful harbour views. There is another Doyles in the Overseas Passenger Terminal at Circular Quay.
✚ Off map to east ✉ 11 Marine Parade, Watsons Bay ☎ 9337 2007 🕐 Daily lunch, dinner 🚍 324, 325
🚢 Watsons Bay

GOLDEN CENTURY ($$)

This busy Chinese restaurant, in the heart of Chinatown, specializes in the freshest seafood.
✚ J7 ✉ 393–9 Sussex Street, Haymarket ☎ 9212 3901
🕐 Daily lunch, dinner
🚇 Central (Railway Square exit)

JORDONS SEAFOOD RESTAURANT ($$)

On the water at Darling Harbour. Serves everything from Atlantic salmon carpaccio to seafood platters.
✚ H6 ✉ Harbourside, Darling Harbour ☎ 9281 3711
🕐 Daily lunch, dinner
🚝 Monorail to Harbourside

LE KIOSK ($$)

It's worth a ferry trip to Manly to experience the seaside cottage ambience and Med/Oz seafood dishes.
✚ Off map to northwest
✉ 1 Marine Parade, Shelly Beach, Manly ☎ 9977 4122
🕐 Sun lunch, Fri–Sun dinner
🚢 Manly

PIER ($$$)

Seared rare, yellow-fin tuna and Queensland reef fish poached in green curry are some of chef Greg Doyle's signature dishes. Superb location.
✚ Off map to east ✉ 594 New South Head Road, Rose Bay ☎ 9363 0927 🕐 Daily lunch, dinner 🚍 324, 325 🚢 Rose Bay

ROCKPOOL ($$–$$$)

Continues its reign as Sydney's best seafood restaurant, chef Neil Perry presenting his signature dishes with flair. The bar serves oysters and other light meals.
✚ bi; J5 ✉ 107 George Street, The Rocks ☎ 9252 1888
🕐 Mon–Fri lunch, Mon–Sat dinner 🚢 Circular Quay

SYDNEY COVE OYSTER BAR ($$)

Light and tasty seafood and oysters on the harbour near the Opera House, with panoramic views. Most seating is outdoors.
✚ ci; K5 ✉ 1 Circular Quay East ☎ 9247 2937 🕐 Daily snacks, lunch and dinner
🚢 Circular Quay

Thai Restaurants

ARUN THAI ($$)

One of Sydney's most reliable Thai restaurants, with a large outdoor dining area. It has a wine licence, but you can also BYO. Close to Kings Cross.

⊕ L6 ⊠ 28 Macleay Street, Potts Point ☎ 9326 9132 🕒 Tue–Sun lunch, daily dinner 🚇 Kings Cross

LONGRAIN ($$$)

Long communal tables are a novelty, but the food is full of taste—try deep-fried barramundi, smoked trout with garlic and pork hock with chilli vinegar.

⊕ J7 ⊠ 85 Commonwealth Street, Surry Hills ☎ 9280 2888 🕒 Mon–Fri lunch, dinner, Sat dinner 🚌 378

PRASIT'S NORTHSIDE THAI ($$)

Rich green, yellow and duck curries are some of the specialties of this sophisticated northside restaurant.

⊕ J2 ⊠ 77 Mount Street, North Sydney ☎ 9957 2271 🕒 Mon–Fri lunch, Tue–Sat dinner 🚇 North Sydney

SAILORS THAI CANTEEN ($$$)

Well-loved by locals. Interesting dishes include roast duck with fresh lychee salad and cured pork grilled in banana leaf.

⊕ bi; J5 ⊠ 106 George Street, The Rocks ☎ 9251 2466 🕒 Daily lunch, dinner 🚇 Circular Quay

THAI ORCHID ($)

Substance over style here—ignore the slightly worn decor—but the curries are always good and the warm salads are popular.

⊕ K7 ⊠ 628 Crown Street, Surry Hills ☎ 9698 2097 🕒 Tue–Sun lunch, dinner 🚌 393, 395

THAI POTHONG ($)

Award-winning authentic Thai cuisine, served in no-frills surrounds in busy King Street.

⊕ 09 🚇 294 King Street, Newtown ☎ 9550 6277 🕒 Tue–Sun lunch, daily dinner 🚇 Newtown

THAI PRINCESS ($$)

Dine and watch the action in this popular dining spot with its open-plan kitchen. Authentic dishes, a quick lunch menu and take-out available.

⊕ K7 ⊠ 118 Crown Street, Darlinghurst ☎ 9332 3284 🕒 Mon–Sat lunch, dinner 🚌 378, 380

TUK TUK THAI ($)

Balmain's most popular Thai eatery is licensed and serves tasty dishes such as hot chilli chicken and *tum yum* soup.

⊕ G4 ⊠ 350 Darling Street, Balmain ☎ 9555 5899 🕒 Wed–Sun lunch, daily dinner 🚌 431 ⛴ Balmain

TUM TUM'S THAI TAKEAWAY($)

This bustling take-out establishment also has a small eating-in area and produces fresh, delicious food. BYO—if you can find a seat.

⊕ K6 ⊠ 199 Darlinghurst Road, Darlinghurst ☎ 9331 5390 🕒 Daily noon–11 🚇 Kings Cross

THAI CUISINE

Sydney is fortunate in that it is positively oversupplied with this wonderful cuisine. Thai food is light and extraordinarily delicious—the combination of very fresh vegetables, meats and seafood with delicate spices and herbs is irresistible. Try the soup known as *tom yum goong*—shirmps seasoned with coriander, lemongrass and chilli: a taste sensation.

Other Asian Restaurants

SYDNEY'S ASIAN RESTAURANTS

Multiculturalism has laid the foundation for an array of Asian restaurants in Sydney. The eating places listed here, from Chinese to Indonesian, are just a sample, but you will also find Singaporean, Nepalese, Burmese, Taiwanese, Javanese, Korean and Laotian. Most Asian restaurants are reasonably priced and many are BYO.

AMARS ($)
Authentic Indian dishes including tandooris, curries and Mughlai cuisine. Will deliver to your hotel room.
✚ J5 ☒ 44a Bridge Street, ☎ 9247 9930 ◷ Mon–Fri lunch, dinner, Sat dinner ⊠ Town Hall

CHINATOWN CENTRE ($)
Sydney has many such inexpensive self-service food halls—choose from excellent Chinese, Malaysian, Thai and others. Licensed.
✚ J7 ☒ 25 Dixon Street, Haymarket ☎ 9212 3335 ◷ Daily 10–10 ⊠ Town Hall

FLAVOUR OF INDIA ($$)
Sydney isn't renowned for its Indian food, but this is one of the best. Another outlet at Glebe.
✚ M7 ☒ 120–8 New South Head Road, Edgecliff ☎ 9326 2659 ◷ Daily dinner ⊠ Edgecliff

IMPERIAL HARBOURSIDE ($$$)
One of Sydney's best Chinese restaurants, with harbour views. Emphasis on seafood.
✚ bi; J4 ☒ 15 Circular Quay West, The Rocks ☎ 9247 7073 ◷ Daily lunch, dinner ⊠ Circular Quay

THE MALAYA ($–$$)
One of the longest-established and best Asian restaurants in town, serving a tempting array of Indonesian, Malaysian and Chinese.
✚ aiii; J6 ☒ 39 Lime Street (Kings Street Wharf) ☎ 9279 1170 ◷ Daily lunch, dinner ⊠ Town Hall

NEPTUNE PALACE ($$$)
Chinese/Malaysian cuisine with dishes such as *lakas*, Malay curries, Penang-style chicken and seafood dishes.
✚ bii; J5 ☒ Level 1, Gateway Building, Corner Pitt & Alfred streets, Circular Quay ☎ 9241 3338 ◷ Daily lunch, dinner ⊠ Circular Quay

OH! CALCUTTA ($$)
This compact restaurant has long been regarded as the home of Sydney's top Indian dishes.
✚ K7 ☒ 251 Victoria Street, Darlinghurst ☎ 9360 3650 ◷ Mon–Sat lunch, dinner ▭ 378, 380

OLD SAIGON ($–$$)
Excellent Vietnamese and Thai food. Cozy atmosphere. Licensed and BYO.
✚ G8 ☒ 107 King Street, Newtown ☎ 9519 5931 ◷ Wed–Fri lunch, daily dinner ⊠ Newtown

RANGOON RACQUET CLUB ($$)
Fine Indian and Sri Lankan food. Excellent tandoori dishes. The decor and ambience is straight out of the British Raj.
✚ H1 ☒ 7/70 Alexander Street, Crows Nest ☎ 9906 4091 ◷ Mon–Fri lunch, daily dinner ▭ 263

THANH BINH ($)
If you like Vietnamese then ponder the 250 dishes on the menu here. Fresh spring rolls are a feature.
✚ G8 ☒ 111 King Street, Newtown ☎ 9557 1175 ◷ Daily lunch, dinner ⊠ Newtown

European Cuisine

BISTRO LULU ($$)
Predominantly French fare with a contemporary twist. Roast rabbit loin, grilled steak and ginger calamari are all popular. The attractive bright interior is open to the street.

⊕ L8 ☒ 257 Oxford Street, Paddington ☎ 9380 6888 🕓 Thu–Sun lunch, daily dinner 🚍 378, 380

BONDI ICEBERGS ($$$)
Fashionable with stunning sea views. The food could best be described as modern Mediterranean with a good selection of seafood dishes. Great wine selection.

⊕ Off map to east ☒ 1 Notts Avenue, Bondi Beach ☎ 9365 9000 🕓 Daily lunch, dinner 🚍 380, 382

BONDI TRATT ($$)
A café-cum-restaurant, which provides tempting Italian food and great views over Bondi Beach.

⊕ Off map to east ☒ 34b Campbell Parade, Bondi Beach ☎ 9365 4303 🕓 Daily 7am–midnight 🚍 380, 382

CAPITAN TORRES ($$)
A popular central establishment with great Spanish dishes, sangria and a lively atmosphere.

⊕ J6 ☒ 73 Liverpool Street ☎ 9264 5574 🕓 Daily lunch, dinner 🚇 Town Hall

COAST ($$$)
Top dining at this trendy establishment, where contemporary Italian cuisine meets Australian influences.

⊕ J6 ☒ Cockle Bay Wharf, Darling Park ☎ 9267 6700 🕓 Mon–Fri lunch, daily dinner 🚇 Town Hall

GELATO BAR ($–$$)
Central and Eastern European food is served at this Bondi institution.

⊕ Off map to east ☒ 140 Campbell Parade, Bondi Beach ☎ 9130 4033 🕓 Daily 8am–midnight 🚍 380, 382

LUCIO'S ($$$)
Top service and top Italian dishes are the trademark of this long-established restaurant.

⊕ L7 ☒ 47 Windsor Street, Paddington ☎ 9380 5996 🕓 Mon–Sat lunch, dinner 🚍 389

ROSSINI'S ($)
Front row position at Circular Quay. True Italian style: Pay first, then choose your food from the display.

⊕ bi; J5 ☒ Shop W5, Circular Quay ☎ 9247 8026 🕓 Daily breakfast, lunch and dinner 🚇 Circular Quay

TABOU ($$)
Soak up the French ambience, including the accordian music and feast on brasserie dishes such as mustard rabbit.

⊕ K7 ☒ 527 Crown Street, Surry Hills ☎ 9319 5682 🕓 Mon–Fri lunch, daily dinner 🚍 380, 382

UN MOMENTO ($$–$$$)
Funky, ultra chic and one of the northside's best eateries, with a large selection from all regions of Italy.

⊕ H1 ☒ 407 Pacific Highway, Crows Nest ☎ 9966 8555 🕓 Tue–Fri lunch, daily dinner 🚇 St. Leonards

AUSTRALIAN WINES

Australian wines have taken the world by storm and are, for many, an integral part of dining out. There have been vineyards in New South Wales and other regions since the 1820s, these producing fine varieties such as Cabernet Sauvignon, Shiraz, Chardonnay and Chablis. There are hundreds of labels, but good winemakers to look for include Lindemans, Rosemount Estate, Houghtons, Wyndham Estate, Henschke, Tyrrells, Penfolds and Wolf Blass.

Cafés

A favourite Sydney occupation is hanging out in a café. The drinks, snacks and meals are generally good value, but many establishments offer far more. Outdoor seating, or a view over Bronte Beach, the Opera House, or harbour are some of the bonuses, while other cafés are in lively areas like The Rocks, Bondi, or inner-city Darlinghurst. Sydney's coffee, thanks to European (particularly Italian) influences, is usually excellent.

BAR COLUZZI ($)

This tiny café, with its alfresco seating, is deservedly popular. The coffee is some of the best around.

✚ K6 ✉ 322 Victoria Street, Darlinghurst ☎ 9380 5420 🕐 Daily 6am–8pm 🚇 Kings Cross

BLACKBIRD ($)

Pasta with an Aussie twist, wood-fired pizza and great salads. The interior is decorated with modern art and 1970s style.

✚ aiv; J6 ✉ Balcony, Cockle Bay Wharf, 201 Sussex Street ☎ 9283 7385 🕐 Daily breakfast, lunch and dinner 🚇 Kings Cross

CAFFE NIKI ($)

Informal and popular with the hip locals who come for the excellent coffee and light meals.

✚ K7 ✉ 544 Bourke Street, Surry Hills ☎ 9319 7517 🕐 Mon–Sat breakfast, lunch and dinner, Sun breakfast, lunch 🚌 380, 382

CAFFE OTTO ($–$$)

This bright and cheerful café serves good soups, pasta and snacks and totally decadent cakes and desserts. BYO.

✚ G7 ✉ 79 Glebe Point Road, Glebe ☎ 9552 1519 🕐 Daily snacks, lunch and dinner 🚌 431

GUMNUT TEA GARDEN ($–$$)

Situated in a tiny cottage, this is one of the nicest places in The Rocks for a break. The all-day menu includes cakes, focaccia, scones, and home-made pies.

✚ bi; J5 ✉ 28 Harrington Street, The Rocks ☎ 9247 9591 🕐 Daily to 5pm 🚇 Circular Quay

GUSTO ($$)

Hearty breakfasts including bacon and eggs and deli lunch special with the works are what makes this café/deli so popular.

✚ L7 ✉ 2a Healy Street, Paddington ☎ 9361 5640 🕐 Daily breakfast, lunch and dinner 🚌 389

HYDE PARK BARRACKS CAFÉ ($$)

Eat inside or in the courtyard at this café, which incorporates the original convict confinement area.

✚ ciii; K6 ✉ Queens Square, Macquarie Street ☎ 9223 1155 🕐 Mon–Fri 10–4, Sat–Sun 11–4 🚇 Martin Place

JACKIE'S ($$)

At the quieter end of Bondi Beach, Jackie's is relaxed and has good water views. Serves snacks and more substantial meals.

✚ Off map to east ✉ 132 Warners Avenue, Bondi Beach ☎ 9300 9812 🕐 Daily breakfast, lunch and dinner 🚌 378, 380, 382, 389

MOS CAFÉ ($$)

Very popular with city workers for breakfast. Lunch and dinner feature great modern creations such as salt-and-pepper squid and chargrilled Junee lamb.

✚ bii; J5 ✉ 37 Phillip Street ☎ 9241 3636 🕐 Mon–Fri breakfast, lunch and dinner, Sat–Sun breakfast, lunch 🚇 Circular Quay

Miscellaneous

STEAKS & BURGERS

DANIELS ($$–$$$)

This is probably the city's best steak restaurant. The good food and the elegant yet friendly atmosphere makes this place a sure winner with patrons.
⊞ J5 ⊠ 1 Bent Street, City ☎ 9251 6977 ⦿ Mon–Fri lunch, dinner ⊟ Wynyard

HARD ROCK CAFÉ ($$)

Extremely noisy, but fun and the rock 'n' roll memorabilia is fascinating. Serves American fare such as hamburgers and French fries.
⊞ K6 ⊠ 121–9 Crown Street, East Sydney ☎ 9331 1116 ⦿ Daily noon–midnight ⊟ 324, 325, 389

NOVELTY

LOWENBRAU ($$)

You'll find traditional Bavarian fare here including chicken schnitzel, port knuckle and cheese *spatzle*. Delicious pastries and a variety of beverages.
⊞ bi; J5 ⊠ 18 Argyle Street, The Rocks ☎ 9247 7785 ⦿ Breakfast, lunch and dinner ⊟ Circular Quay

SYDNEY TOWER ($$–$$$)

A revolving restaurant. Two levels of à la carte dining right in the heart of the CBD, with ever-changing views of the city.
⊞ J6 ⊠ Gallery Level, 100 Market Street, Centrepoint ☎ 8223 3800 ⦿ Daily lunch, dinner ⊟ Town Hall

PRE-THEATRE

AQUA LUNA ($$$)

Just a few minutes' walk from the Opera House. Modern Italian specialties including various antipasti and adventurous pasta dishes.
⊞ ci; K5 ⊠ Shop 8, Opera Quays, 7 Macquarie Street ☎ 9251 0311 ⦿ Mon–Fri lunch, daily dinner ⊟ Circular Quay

FIREFLY ($$)

Informal indoor/outdoor café-cum-wine bar patronized by the Wharf Theatre crowd. The development of the Walsh Bay area has created a great new atmosphere.
⊞ J4 ⊠ Pier 7, 17 Hickson Road, Walsh Bay ☎ 9241 2031 ⦿ Daily breakfast, lunch and dinner ⊟ 431

BAR/PUB FOOD

WATSONS BAY HOTEL ($)

This pub offers barbecued seafood and the same harbour outlook as its more expensive neighbour, Doyles (► 66).
⊞ Off map to east ⊠ 1 Military Road, Watsons Bay ☎ 9337 4299 ⦿ Daily lunch ⊟ 324, 325 ⊟ Watsons Bay

VEGETARIAN

ROY'S FAMOUS ($$)

A good vegetarian eatery, offering inventive, tasty and filling meals. BYO and licensed.
⊞ div; L6 ⊠ 176 Victoria Street, Potts Point ☎ 9357 3579 ⦿ Daily breakfast, lunch and dinner ⊟ Kings Cross

FOOD AFLOAT

There is no better way to experience the harbour's magic than by dining on the water. Although the cuisine of these floating restaurants rarely reaches gourmet standards, lunch or dinner cruises are understandably popular. Operators include Captain Cook Cruises (lunches and dinners ☎ 9206 1122), Matilda Cruises (lunchtime barbecues ☎ 9264 7377) and Sydney Ferries offer morning, afternoon and evening cruises with onboard food and expert commentary.

Australiana & Souvenirs

AUSSIE DESIGN

Sydney's designers have been instrumental in setting an aesthetic agenda for the city and none more so than Ken Done (✉ 123–5 George Street ☎ 9251 6099). Done's bright, simple designs adorn clothing, scarves, bags, prints and jewellery. Mambo (✉ 17 Oxford Street, Paddington ☎ 9331 8034) stocks bright surf and streetwear carrying over-the-top designs from the talented Reg Mombassa. Makers Mark (✉ 72A Castlereagh Street ☎ 9231 6800) sells work from over 100 of Australia's top designers and jewellers with finely crafted objects in glass, wood, porcelain and silver. Funky, translucent and cheerful best describes the jewellery and homewares at Dinosaur Designs (✉ 339 Oxford Street, Paddington ☎ 9361 3776).

AUSTRALIANA

If you are looking for souvenirs to take home, go for high-quality Australiana. You will find everything from jazzy beachwear to sheepskin products, books on every aspect of Australia, Aboriginal crafts and superb gemstones and jewellery (► 75).

THE AUSTRALIAN GEOGRAPHIC SHOP

Operated by a popular magazine, this shop sells unusual and environmentally friendly Australian books, gifts and sturdy outdoor clothing.
✚ biv; J6 ✉ Shop C14, Sydney Arcade, Pitt Street Mall ☎ 9221 8299 🚇 St. James

AUSTRALIAN IMAGE CRAFT

An excellent range of glass, ceramics, prints, enamels, opal and gold jewellery, basketry and art to wear, including silk painted and woven garments .
✚ bi; J5 ✉ Shop 2, Metcalfe Arcade, The Rocks ☎ 9241 1673 🚇 Circular Quay

BLUE GUM DESIGN

A general Australiana shop with souvenirs and clothing, but specializing in Aboriginal items such as didgeridoos (lessons are available).
✚ biii; J5 ✉ Wynyard Centre, 301 George Street ☎ 9262 6991 🚇 Wynyard

DONE ART & DESIGN

Ken Done's 'art to wear' has become a vibrant Australian symbol and this shop stocks his popular resortwear and homeware. The nearby Ken Done Gallery, at 1 Hickson Road, sells his paintings.
✚ bi; J5 ✉ 123 George Street, The Rocks ☎ Freephone 9251 6099 🚇 Circular Quay

NATURALLY AUSTRALIAN

Finely crafted wooden boxes, platters, tableware, furniture and sculptures. The majority of pieces are handmade by Australian crafts-people using indigenous timber such as Australian red cedar.
✚ bi; J5 ✉ 43 Circular Quay West, The Rocks ☎ 9247 1531 🚇 Circular Quay

R.M. WILLIAMS

The legendary Bushman's Outfitters sells Australian country and Outback clothing, including moleskin pants, leather boots and Drizabone oilskin coats. High quality is assured.
✚ biii; J6 ✉ 389 George Street, The Rocks ☎ 9262 2228 🚇 Town Hall

SHEEPSKIN SHOP

Since 1958 this Sydney institution has been selling Australian-made skin and leather products of excellent quality.
✚ bi; J5 ✉ 139 George Street, The Rocks ☎ 9241 1099 🚇 Circular Quay

SOUNDS AUSTRALIAN

A specialist shop offering Australian classical, folk, jazz and Aboriginal music in the form of CDs, tapes and sheet music, as well as books on music.
✚ bi; J5 ✉ The Rocks Centre, 10–26 Playfair Street, The Rocks ☎ 9247 4677 🚇 Circular Quay

WEISS ART

Distinctive black and white line-drawings of Aussie animals decorate clothing, homeware and other goods.
✚ bi; J5 ✉ 85 George Street, The Rocks ☎ 9241 3819 🚇 Circular Quay

Opals, Gems & Jewellery

DINOSAUR DESIGNS
Silver and semi-precious stones are used in offbeat and modern designs in this central jewellery shop.

✚ biii; J6 ✉ Shop 73, Strand Arcade, Pitt Street Mall ☎ 9223 2953 🚇 St. James

THE FAMILY JEWELS
Beautifully designed contemporary gold, silver and other jewellery, set with semi-precious stones such as amethyst and turquoise.

✚ K7 ✉ 46 Oxford Street, Paddington ☎ 9331 6647
🚌 378, 380, 382

FLAME OPALS
One of Sydney's many opal stockists, selling everything from the white milk variety to black Lightning Ridge opals from the remote New South Wales town of that name. The stones are also sold set in gold or silver.

✚ bi; J5 ✉ 119 George Street, The Rocks ☎ 9247 3446
🚇 Circular Quay

HARDY BROTHERS
An Australian gem specialist, featuring exquisite Broome South Sea pearls, Argyle diamonds and fine opals. You will also find the best silverware, china and a range of other items here.

✚ biii; J6 ✉ Skygarden, 77 Castlereagh Street ☎ 9232 2422 🚇 St. James

MAKERS MARK
Beautifully crafted Australian jewellery and other objects, including an extensive range of Argyle diamonds. You can buy ready-made pieces or design your own.

✚ biii; J5 ✉ Chifley Tower, Chifley Square ☎ 9231 6800
🚇 Martin Place

OPAL FIELDS
Sydney's largest opal specialist also sells unusual gifts. There is a museum dedicated entirely to opals on the premises.

✚ bi; J5 ✉ 151 George Street, The Rocks ☎ 9247 6800
🚇 Circular Quay

PASPALEY PEARLS
Sydney's South Sea pearl specialist, with outlets in Paris and New York. Paspaley's northern Australian pearling company is regarded as the source of the finest pearls in the world.

✚ biii; J6 ✉ 142 King Street
☎ 9232 7633 🚇 Martin Place

PERRI JEWELLERS
Another good quality establishment, selling jewellery crafted from gold, pearls, opals, diamonds and other stones. The company has won several prestigious De Beers design awards.

✚ biii; J6 ✉ Shop 708, MLC Centre, corner of King and Castlereagh streets
☎ 9231 1088
🚇 Martin Place

VERN JEWELS
Unique works utilizing a variety of attractive gemstones.

✚ L7 ✉ 36b Oxford Street, Paddington ☎ 9361 3669
🚌 380, 382

SHOPPING HOURS

Shopping hours are generally 9–5.30 on weekdays and 9–4 on Saturdays, but many shops, particularly in tourist areas, are open daily. It is always best to check by phoning beforehand.

75

Markets

BARGAIN SHOPPING

The best shopping bargains are found at sales times—after Christmas and into January and again at the end of winter in July and August. You can shop for budget clothing at any time in Surry Hills, Sydney's rag trade area, and at Redfern, where designer outfits and other clothes are very reasonably priced. Inner-west Newtown (especially King Street) offers bargains in second-hand clothing and many other items. In the city, be sure to check out Market City near Chinatown for bargains galore from the hundreds of stall operators who trade here.

BALMAIN MARKET

With shoppers ranging from punks to ageing hippies, this market (held in the grounds of an old church) has a pleasant community feel. Come and browse for arts and crafts and, in the church hall, try the vegetarian food.

➕ G4 ✉ Corner of Darling Street and Curtis Road, Balmain ☎ 9818 2674 🕐 Sat 8.30–4 🚌 433, 442 🚢 Darling Street

BONDI BEACH MARKET

One of Sydney's newer markets, the outdoor Bondi sells arts and crafts, clothing and an interesting range of second-hand goods.

➕ Off map to east ✉ Corner of Campbell Parade and Warners Avenue, Bondi Beach ☎ 9315 8988 🕐 Sun 9–4 🚌 380, 382

GLEBE MARKETS

Around 200 outdoor stalls with plenty of clothing and fashion items, crafts and collectables. Many interesting shops and some great cafés are nearby.

➕ H7 ✉ Glebe Public School, Glebe Point Road, Glebe ☎ 4237 7499 🕐 Sat 9–4 🚌 431, 433

PADDINGTON BAZAAR

This is the trendiest market in town. Mostly clothes, arts, crafts and jewellery at some good prices. The street performers are often very entertaining.

➕ L8 ✉ Corner of Oxford and Newcombe streets, Paddington ☎ 9331 2923 🕐 Sat 10–4 🚌 378, 380, 382

PADDY'S MARKETS

Sydney's biggest and oldest market, with more than 1,000 stalls under cover, selling everything from clothes and books to jewellery and vegetables. Great for bargain hunters.

➕ J7 ✉ Corner of Thomas and Hay streets, Haymarket ☎ 1300 361 589 🕐 Fri–Sun 9–4.30 🚇 Central (Railway Square exit)

THE ROCKS MARKET

More than 150 stalls sell gifts, homeware, antiques and jewellery in The Rocks; there are also plenty of streetside cafés, as well as free entertainment.

➕ bi; J4 ✉ George Street, The Rocks ☎ 9240 8717 🕐 Sat, Sun 10–5 🚆 Circular Quay

THE SYDNEY ANTIQUE CENTRE

Not so much a market as a treasure trove of antiques. Around 60 shops sell jewellery, furniture, glassware, prints, books and many other items.

➕ K8 ✉ 531 South Dowling Street, Surry Hills ☎ 9361 3244 🕐 Daily 10–6 🚌 373, 374, 394 to Anzac Parade

SYDNEY FISH MARKET

Come to admire (and buy if you are going to a barbecue!) the extraordinary range of fresh seafood and to sample the great fish and French fries. Fruit, vegetables and deli items are also on sale.

➕ H6 ✉ Blackwattle Bay, Pyrmont ☎ 9660 1611 🕐 Daily 7–4 🚌 441, 501

Books

ARIEL BOOKSELLERS

This stylish establishment is a delightful place to shop. There is a particularly good photography and art section.

🞣 K7 ✉ 42 Oxford Street, Paddington ☎ 9332 4512
🕐 Daily until midnight
🚌 378, 380, 382

DENKELOUW BOOKDEALERS

Mostly second-hand and rare books. Has a good coffee bar upstairs.

🞣 K7 ✉ 19 Oxford Street, Paddington ☎ 9360 3200
🕐 Daily until midnight
🚌 378, 380, 382

BORDERS BOOKS

Carries an extensive range of books, CDs and DVDs. The in-store café is popular.

🞣 biv; J6 ✉ Skygarde, Pitt Street Mall ☎ 9235 2433
🚇 Town Hall

COLLINS BOOKSELLERS

A mega store whose stock includes a comprehensive collection of Australian fiction and non-fiction.

🞣 H7 ✉ The Broadway Shopping Centre, Glebe
☎ 9566 1095 🚇 Central

DYMOCKS

Sydney's largest bookshop stocks books on every imaginable topic. The Australian section near the entrance is very good and the best place to peruse what is in the country's bestseller list.

🞣 biv; J6 ✉ 424–30 George Street ☎ 9235 0155
🚇 Town Hall

GLEEBOOKS

An excellent and long-established bookshop in the inner-west suburb of Glebe, close to the University of Sydney. Great for browsing.

🞣 G7 ✉ 49 Glebe Point Road, Glebe ☎ 9660 2333 🚌 431
✉ Also at 191 Glebe Point Road (see next entry)

GLEEBOOKS

This branch specializes in second-hand and children's books.

🞣 G7 ✉ 191 Glebe Point Road, Glebe ☎ 9552 2526
🚌 431

LESLEY MCKAY'S BOOKSHOP

This beautifully laid-out store has varied Australian topics. A children's bookshop is across the road and the Nicholas Pounder shop (devoted to modern first editions) is upstairs.

🞣 M7 ✉ 346 New South Head Road, Double Bay
☎ 9327 1354 🚌 324, 325

STATE LIBRARY OF NSW

If you are particularly interested in Australian history or literature, this is your best bet.

🞣 ciii; K5 ✉ Macquarie Street
☎ 9273 1414 🚇 Martin Place

THE TRAVEL BOOKSHOP

If you need maps, books or travel literature on virtually any destination in the world, including Australia itself, a visit here, with its well-informed staff, is definitely worth while.

🞣 J6 ✉ 175 Liverpool Street
☎ 9261 8200 🚇 Museum

BOOKS ON AUSTRALIA

If you are looking for a worthwhile souvenir of your visit, there are dozens of high-quality photographic books on Sydney and Australia in the city's many bookshops. For a well-written, no-holds-barred account of the nation's early history, *The Fatal Shore* by Robert Hughes is unbeatable. Another interesting historical book is *The Road to Botany Bay* by Paul Carter, while you can learn much about Aboriginal Australia by reading any of Jennifer Isaacs' beautifully illustrated books.

Food & Wine

AUSTRALIAN DELICACIES

While in Sydney, don't fail to sample some Australian delicacies. Cheeses, particularly those from Tasmania, are wonderful–try King Island cheddar and camembert. Seafood is relatively inexpensive and incredibly varied–everything from Sydney rock oysters to Tasmanian smoked salmon– and most fish shops will cook your selection. Exotic Aussie-grown fruits and vegetables such as mangoes, bananas, avocados and pineapples are plentiful. Other Australian specialties are macadamia nuts, Tasmanian honey and wines.

THE AUSTRALIAN WINE CENTRE

Choose from more than 1,000 Australian wines, including a good range of vintages. They will happily deliver to your hotel, or arrange overseas delivery.

➕ bii; J5 ✉ Goldfields House, 3/1 Alfred Street ☎ 9247 2755 🚇 Circular Quay

DAVID JONES FOOD HALL

The lower level of this store is the city's most exclusive food shop. You will find wonderful produce here, including delicatessen lines, Australian wines, beers, cheeses, meats, seafood, fruit and vegetables.

➕ biv; J6 ✉ Market Street store, corner of Market and Castlereagh streets ☎ 9266 5544 🚇 St. James

FARMERS' MARKET AT FOX STUDIOS

Much of the fresh produce here is direct from the grower so it is well worth the 15-minute bus ride from the CBD. (Wed–Sat only 10–4).

➕ L8 ✉ Driver Avenue, Moore Park ☎ 9383 4163 🚌 371, 373, 376, 377

JUST WILLIAM CHOCOLATES

This tiny shop, just off Paddington's Oxford Street, sells exquisite hand-made chocolates.

➕ L7 ✉ 4 William Street, Paddington ☎ 9331 5468 🚌 378, 380, 382

MACRO

Alternative food tastes are well catered for at this hip health food shop that also dispenses homeopathic remedies.

➕ N8 ✉ 31–35 Oxford Street, Bondi Junction ☎ 9389 7611 🚇 Bondi Junction

THE NUT SHOP

One of Sydney's hidden treasures. Fresh nuts including macadamias, dried fruits and chocolate-coated treats. Located in the elegant 19th-century Strand Arcade.

➕ biv; J6 ✉ Ground Floor, Strand Arcade ☎ 9231 3038 🚇 Town Hall

PARIS CAKE SHOP

Wonderfully fresh cakes and pastries, including French specialties such as brioche, *pain au chocolat* and croissants.

➕ Off map to east ✉ 91 Bondi Road, Bondi ☎ 9387 2496 🚌 380, 382

THAI-KEE SUPERMARKET

An Asian supermarket in Chinatown, featuring exotic fruit and vegetables, a butcher's section and every kind of spice and ingredient for Chinese, Malaysian, Thai and Vietnamese cooking.

➕ J7 ✉ 393 Sussex Street ☎ 9281 2202 🚇 Central

VINTAGE CELLARS

One of the city's best package shops (Australians call them bottle shops), with a high-quality range of Australian and imported wines, beers and spirits.

➕ M7 ✉ 396 New South Head Road, Double Bay ☎ 9327 1333 🚌 324, 325

Other Shops

THE ABC SHOP

Operated by the Australian Broadcasting Corporation, this shop offers books, videos, music and audio cassettes, CDs, toys and clothes relating to Australian TV and radio shows.

✚ biv; J6 ✉ Shop 48, First Floor, Queen Victoria Building, George Street ☎ 9286 3726 🚇 Town Hall

ADRIENNE & MISS BONNEY

The finest of the fine at this exclusive baby boutique. Exquisite hand-made clothes, nursery gifts, an array of soft toys and bedtime garments.

✚ M7 ✉ 20 Cross Street, Double Bay ☎ 9363 1723 🚌 324, 325

BONDI SURF CO.

Everything for the surfer. You can rent surfboards and boogie boards to try out in the Bondi surf and buy beachwear, including the popular Billabong, Rip Curl and Hot Tuna brands.

✚ Off map to east ✉ Shop 2, 72–6 Campbell Parade, Bondi Beach ☎ 9365 0870 🚌 9380, 382

COUNTRY ROAD

An Australian international success story, Country Road also has branches in the Queen Victoria Building and the Skygarden Centre (as well as overseas). Countrified his and hers casual clothes and home furnishings. Popular with bush and city dwellers alike.

✚ J6 ✉ Corner of Pitt and King streets ☎ 9394 1818 🚇 Martin Place

FOLKWAYS

One of Sydney's finest DVD and CD shops, selling everything from classical to comedy, but with a particularly good selection of Australian, Aboriginal, blues and world music.

✚ L7 ✉ 282 Oxford Street, Paddington ☎ 9361 3980 🚌 378, 380, 382

MARGO RICHARDS ANTIQUES

Large selection of antique jewellery, old clothing, shawls, fans, parasols and decorative arts.

✚ bi; J5 ✉ 27 Nurszes Walk, The Rocks ☎ 9252 2855 🚇 Circular Quay

STRAND HATTERS

Bill Clinton has one, Greg Norman plays golf in his and Australian cattlemen wouldn't be seen without one—the genuine Akubra rabbit-skin hat. Strand Hatters certainly has the best range.

✚ biii; J6 ✉ Shop 8, Strand Arcade, 412 George Street ☎ 9231 6884 🚇 Town Hall

WILDERNESS SOCIETY SHOP

You can help support the conservation of Australian wild places by shopping for a range of gifts, books and herbal products.

✚ biv; J6 ✉ Shop C3, Centrepoint, Castlereagh Street ☎ 9233 4674 🚇 Town Hall

SYDNEY LIFESTYLE

For a taste of Sydney's diverse lifestyle, combine a harbour crossing (► 20) with a visit to the northern beaches' premier shopping complex, Warringah Mall (✉ Pittwater Road, Brookvale 🕐 Mon–Wed, Fri 9–5.30, Thu 9–9, Sat 9–4, Sun 10–4). Just 30 minutes from the city by JetCat and bus and 10 minutes from Manly (► 37) are its 170 specialist shops, plus branches of the department stores David Jones (► 72) and Myer, as well as relaxed outdoor and indoor shopping with garden courtyards, open-air cafés, cinemas, restaurants and free entertainment.

Theatres & Classical Performances

CLASSICAL SYDNEY

Sydney offers an excellent array of opera, ballet and classical music. Don't miss seeing a performance at the Sydney Opera House (see entry this page)—the Sydney Symphony Orchestra, Australian Chamber Orchestra, Sydney Philharmonia, the Australian Ballet and Australian Opera all perform regularly. The Sydney Theatre Company and Sydney Dance Company can often be seen at the Opera House Drama Theatre, while the complex's Playhouse offers a variety of theatre shows. Classical music concerts also take place at the Town Hall, the City Recital Hall in Angel Place and the Conservatorium of Music on Macquarie Street (☎ 9351 1342).

ABORIGINAL DANCE

Bangarra Dance Company, which fuses contemporary and traditional dance routines into dramatic and exciting performances, can be seen at the Theatre Royal and the Opera House (☎ 9251 5333 for details).

BELVOIR STREET THEATRE

Compny B, a long-established theatre company, performs some of Australia's newest productions and has fostered such talents as Geoffrey Rush.
🞠 K8 ✉ 25 Belvoir Street, Surry Hills ☎ 9667 3444
🞠 Central

CAPITOL THEATRE

Refurbishment has made the historic 2,000-seat Capitol, dating from 1928, Sydney's most glorious performance space. This is the home of musicals and major theatrical events, and highly recommended.
🞠 J7 ✉ 13 Campbell Street, Haymarket ☎ 9266 4800 for performance information
🞠 Central (Railway Square exit)

LYRIC THEATRE

Managed by Andrew Lloyd Webber's company, this new theatre presents a variety of internationally acclaimed theatrical performances.
🞠 H6 ✉ 20–80 Pyrmont Street, Pyrmont ☎ 9777 9000 for performance information
🞠 Star City

SEYMOUR THEATRE CENTRE

There are three theatres here—for drama, dance and chamber music—plus good restaurant and bar facilities.
🞠 H8 ✉ Corner of Cleveland Street and City Road, Chippendale ☎ 9364 9400 for performance information 🖥 422–428

STATE THEATRE

This ornate 2,000-seat theatre is the venue for musicals, ballet, the Sydney Film Festival and performances of live music. The State dates from 1929 and is National Trust-classified because of its splendid art-deco interior.
🞠 biv; J6 ✉ 49 Market Street ☎ 13 6100 for performance information 🞠 Town Hall

SYDNEY OPERA HOUSE

Despite its name, this famous building is not just a home for operatic productions. It contains four main performance spaces, including the 2,690-seat concert hall and the smaller opera venue (➤ panel). For more information (➤ 26).
🞠 ci; K4 ✉ Bennelong Point ☎ Events information 9250 7209. Box office 9250 7777
🕔 Daily; closed Good Fri, 25 Dec
🞠 Circular Quay

THEATRE ROYAL

This modern, well-appointed, central performance venue specializes in putting on long-running musicals.
🞠 biii; J6 ✉ MLC Centre, King Street ☎ 13 6166 for performance information
🞠 Martin Place

WHARF THEATRE

The intimate home of the excellent Sydney Theatre Company, which also performs at the nearby Sydney Theatre and in The Dram Theatre at the Opera House.
🞠 J4 ✉ Pier 4, Hickson Road, Walsh Bay ☎ 9250 1777
🕔 Shows Mon–Sat
🞠 Circular Quay

Modern Live Music

ANNANDALE HOTEL
This lively hotel is one of the best places to sample some of Australia's up-and-coming bands.
🔶 F8 ✉ 105 Johnston Street, Annandale ☎ 9550 1078
🕐 Daily 🚌 413, 435, 461

THE BASEMENT
This famous, long-established club is the city's best venue for live blues, jazz and funk at reasonable prices. The atmosphere is great and the good value restaurant serves nice food.
🔶 biii; J5 ✉ 7 Macquarie Place ☎ 9251 2797 🕐 Daily
🚇 Circular Quay

ENMORE THEATRE
This former playhouse now hosts top-line visiting entertainment, including rock bands, theatrical dance spectaculars and stand-up comedy acts.
🔶 F9 ✉ 130 Enmmore Road, Enmore ☎ 9550 3666
🕐 Most nights 🚇 Newtown

EXCELSIOR HOTEL
One of Sydney's bargain music venues. Rockabilly, blues and rock performed most nights.
🔶 J7 ✉ 64 Foveaux Street, Surry Hills ☎ 9211 4945 for performances 🕐 Most nights
🚇 Central

HOPETOUN HOTEL
Many bands have had their start here and, while the quality may vary, this pub is still worth checking out.
🔶 K7 ✉ 416 Bourke Street. Surry Hills ☎ 9361 5257
🕐 Most nights 🚇 Central

THE METRO
The Metro, which is in the same complex as the excellent Dendy Cinema (► 85, panel), is a great venue to catch local rock, folk and other types of bands. Dance, comedy and other performances also feature occasionally.
🔶 J6 ✉ 624 George Street ☎ 9287 2000 for performance information 🚇 Town Hall

PONTOON
Trendy bar overlooking Darling Harbour with futuristic interior decor. Music varies, but Sundays feature jazz from 3–6pm. Thursday, Friday and Saturday you can dance to a thumping sound system.
🔶 aiv; J6 ✉ Cockle Bay Wharf, Darling Harbour ☎ 9267 7099 🕐 Daily noon–late
🚇 Town Hall

SOUP PLUS
A moderately priced restaurant with good soups, snacks and pasta, plus free jazz. Great value.
🔶 biii; J6 ✉ 383 George Street ☎ 9299 7728
🕐 Mon–Sat from lunchtime
🚇 Town Hall, Wynyard

SYDNEY ENTERTAINMENT CENTRE
Sydney's largest entertainment venue hosts everything from concerts by touring international rock groups to indoor tennis and basketball matches.
🔶 J7 ✉ Harbour Street, Haymarket ☎ 9320 4200
🕐 Performances most days
🚇 Monorail to Haymarket

BUYING A TICKET
There are several ways of obtaining tickets for theatre, live music and other events. You can visit the box offices, purchase via credit card from the ticketing agency Ticketek (☎ 9266 4800) or buy discounted tickets from Halftix (☎ 9279 0855). This half-price service operates from 91 York Street or on www.halftix.com.au
🕐 Mon–Fri 9.30–5.30, Sat 10–3.30

Hotels & Bars

SYDNEY WATERING HOLES

Drinking is a very popular pastime in Sydney and there are countless bars and pubs to visit. In addition to the well-known Foster's and VB beers, there are more unusual brands such as Redback, Hahn and Coopers. Australia's local spirit is Bundaberg rum 'Bundy', available in underproof and the lethal overproof varieties. Beer is generally served in 'middies' (284ml/10fl oz glasses) and larger 'schooners'. Bars and pubs, some of which are located in hotels, are licensed to trade for varying hours each day but are generally open until at least 11pm, while nightclubs and discos stay open longer.

BAR EUROPA

Join the locals at this club-like basement bar complex where DJs are on hand to entertain. Snug booths and good cocktails make for a great time. Despite its name it has an element of New York cool.

✚ bii; J5 ✉ 88 Elizabeth Street, City ☎ 9232 3377 🕐 Tue–Sat 8pm–late 🚇 Wynyard

BROOKLYN HOTEL

The Brooklyn is one of central Sydney's best and trendiest hotels, with contemporary decor and a good dining room.

✚ bii; J5 ✉ Corner of Grosvenor and George streets ☎ 9247 6744 🕐 Daily 🚇 Wynyard

BURDEKIN HOTEL

This popular hotel in Darlinghurst has a large bar on the Oxford Street side and the more intimate, expensive Dug Out Bar on Liverpool Street with its flattering low lighting and friendly, attentive staff.

✚ K7 ✉ 2 Oxford Street, Darlinghurst ☎ 9331 3066 🕐 Daily 🚇 Museum

THE HORIZON

This pricey 36th-floor cocktail bar in one of the city's top hotels provides elegance with astounding views of the harbour.

✚ aii; J5 ✉ Shangri-la Hotel, 176 Cumberland Street, The Rocks ☎ 9250 6000 🕐 Daily 🚇 Circular Quay

HOTEL BONDI

After a day on the beach this is a great place to mix with the locals, listen to live bands, play pool or just hang out.

✚ off map to East ✉ 178 Campbell Parade, Bondi Beach ☎ 9130 3271 🕐 Daily 🚌 380, 382

LORD DUDLEY

A very popular English-style pub that (unusually for Sydney) serves beer in pint and half-pint tankards. The downstairs eating area is worth a visit, too.

✚ M7 ✉ 236 Jersey Road, Woollahra ☎ 9327 5399 🕐 Daily 🚌 389

LORD NELSON BREWERY HOTEL

A visit to Sydney's oldest pub is a must—drinks have been served in this sandstone building since 1842 and the atmosphere is wonderful. The counter meals are also good.

✚ ai; J4 ✉ 19 Kent Street, Millers Point ☎ 9251 4044 🕐 Daily 🚌 431, 432, 433

MERCANTILE HOTEL

This high-spirited Irish pub, established in 1915, is located in the cheerful Rocks hotel, famous for its art-deco wall tiles, Irish music and draught Guinness.

✚ bi; J4 ✉ 25 George Street, The Rocks ☎ 9247 3570 🕐 Daily 🚇 Circular Quay

TANK STREAM BAR

See and be seen at this bar preferred by workers from the City keen on forgetting the day's toil.

✚ bii; J5 ✉ 1 Tank Stream Way ☎ 9240 3000 🕐 Mon–Fri 4pm–midnight 🚇 Circular Quay

Dance Clubs

ARQ

Ultra-chic design combined with a variety of dance music. It is best to check the information line as things change regularly at this gay club.

➕ K7 ✉ 16 Flinders Street, Taylor Square ☎ 9380 8700
🕐 Thu–Sat 9pm–closure varies
🚌 378, 380

THE CAVE

Fridays are funk, soul, groove, hip hop and R 'n' B. Saturday nights feature DJs playing a mix of funk, soul and R 'n' B.

➕ H6 ✉ Star City Casino, Pirrama Road, Pyrmont
☎ 9566 4755 🕐 Fri–Sat 9pm–6am 🚌 Star City Light Rail

DCM

Dance with no limits at this hot club where several chill-out rooms offer après dance relaxation.

➕ K7 ✉ 355 Oxford Street, Darlinghurst ☎ 9267 7380
🕐 Fri–Sat 10pm–6am
🚌 378, 380, 382

GAS

One of the best clubs in the CBD (Central Business District). A variety of music and it's the best place to catch hot new bands-about-town.

➕ J7 ✉ 477 Pitt Street, Haymarket ☎ 9211 3088
🕐 Thu–Sat 10pm–6am
🚌 Central

GOODBAR

Formerly The Freezer and Hip Hop Club— loud, packed and hyper-hip. Free Wednesday.

Thursday is funk, Friday the music is canned, Saturday is the hip icebox and on Sunday it is soul.

➕ K7 ✉ 11a Oxford Street, Paddington ☎ 9360 6759
🕐 Wed–Sat 9pm–3am
🚌 373, 374, 380, 382

HOME

Several bars, views of Darling Harbour and, best of all, three levels of dance featuring funk, house, techno and garage.

➕ J6 ✉ Cockle Bay Wharf, Darling Harbour ☎ 9266 0600
🕐 Fri–Sat 11pm–6am
🚌 Town Hall

ICEBOX

A mix of rhythm and blues, hip hop and funk, with different raves on different nights. The Milkbar offers a retro atmosphere and has a camp following.

➕ L6 ✉ 2 Kellet Street, Kings Cross ☎ 9331 0058
🕐 Wed–Sun 🚌 Kings Cross

MIDNIGHT SHIFT

One of Sydney's most popular gay bars and discos. Not for everyone, but a great place to visit if the gay scene interests you (▶ panel).

➕ K7 ✉ 85 Oxford Street, Darlinghurst ☎ 9360 4319
🕐 Nightly 🚌 Museum

SOHO

This is one for the serious clubber who likes to dress up to dance. Polar cool is needed to get past the doorman.

➕ L6 ✉ 171 Victoria Street, Potts Point ☎ 9358 6511
🕐 Nightly 🚌 Kings Cross

GAY AND LESBIAN SYDNEY

Sydney is the home of the world's largest gay and lesbian parade–the Mardi Gras–that takes place each February/ March. The area around lower Oxford Street (sometimes referred to as The Great Gay Way) is the heart of this alternative scene. Many hotels, bars and clubs here cater to gays and lesbians; popular venues include the Midnight Shift (see entry this page), the Lord Roberts Hotel (✉ 64 Stanley Street, East Sydney) and the Newtown Hotel (✉ 174 King Street, Newtown).

Sports

WATERSPORTS

Sydney's location offers unlimited opportunities for watersports. You can windsurf from Rose Bay (☎ 9371 7036), go diving at Coogee (☎ 9665 6333) or sail with the Northside Sailing School (☎ 9969 3972). Weekend surf carnivals, where lifesavers from opposing clubs compete, are held at beaches such as Bondi and Manly from October to March and you can watch competitive sailing on the harbour. The most exciting races, between 6-m (19-ft) long skiffs, are held on Saturday afternoons from mid-September to April–full details are available from the Sydney Flying Squadron (☎ 9955 8350).

AUSSIE STADIUM

Rugby league, rugby union and football (soccer) are played in this ultra-modern stadium. You can watch a match during winter, or join one of the guided tours—contact Sportspace Tours (☎ 9380 0383).
✚ L8 ✉ Driver Avenue, Moore Park ☎ 9360 6601, 🚌 Tours Mon–Sat 🚊 372, 373, 377, 393, 394, 396

CENTENNIAL PARK

The perfect venue for cycling, horse riding, walking, rollerblading and jogging on the edge of central Sydney. Horses and equipment can be rented (► 48).
✚ M8 ✉ Off Oxford Street, Woollahra ☎ 9331 5056
🕐 Daily during daylight hours
🚊 378, 380, 382

COOPER PARK TENNIS COURTS

Scenically, there is no better place for tennis than this bushland spot between Bondi Junction and Double Bay.
✚ N8 ✉ Suttie Road, Double Bay ☎ 9389 9259
🕐 Daily 🚆 Bondi Junction, then bus 330

MOORE PARK GOLF CLUB

An easily accessible golf club not far from the city centre, that offers an 18-hole course, a day and night driving range, and all the normal facilities for very reasonable rates.
✚ K9 ✉ Cleveland Street, Moore Park ☎ 9663 1064
🕐 Daily (driving range until 8pm) 🚊 373, 374, 377, 394

NORTH SYDNEY OLYMPIC POOL

This harbourside pool has views of the Harbour Bridge and Opera House. Open air in summer, but covered by a 'bubble' in cooler months.
✚ J3 ✉ Alfred Street, Milsons Point ☎ 9955 2309
🕐 Mon–Fri 6am–9pm, Sat–Sun 7–7 🚆 Milsons Point

RANDWICK RACECOURSE

This famous eastern suburbs racecourse offers more than 50 horse-racing meetings each year.
✚ L10 ✉ Alison Road, Randwick ☎ 9663 8425
🚊 372, 373, 374, 377

SYDNEY CRICKET GROUND

The famed SCG is the home of first class cricket in New South Wales. Test and one-day matches are played in summer, or you can visit the stadium and its Cricket Museum on a tour—contact Sportspace Tours (☎ 9380 0383).
✚ L8 ✉ Driver Avenue, Moore Park ☎ 9360 6601, match information 0055 63132
🕐 Tours Mon–Sat 🚊 372, 373, 377, 393, 394, 396

SYDNEY ENTERTAINMENT CENTRE

The home of Sydney basketball, whose season runs from April to September.
✚ J7 ✉ Harbour Street, Haymarket ☎ 9266 4800
🕐 Usually Fri and Sat, Apr–Sep
🚝 Monorail to Haymarket

Other Entertainment

See also Architecture & Interiors (➤ 56–57), Free Attractions (➤ 62) Sydney Harbour dinner cruises (➤ 71, panel).

AUSTRALIAN REPTILE PARK

Located at Gosford on the Central Coast less than an hour's drive north of Sydney. On show are reptiles of all kinds, including crocodiles, snakes and the wonderful Galapagos tortoises, which can weigh up to 180kg (400lbs) and live as long as 160 years. Also koalas, kangaroos, emus and parrots and Australia's only spider zoo.
✚ Off map to north ✉ Pacific Highway, Somersby ☎ 4340 1022 ⏰ Daily 9–5

CITY FARM

This is a great place for the family to share some experiences of bush life, including shearing sheep, tractor rides and milking demonstrations. Café, milk-bar style take-out and lots of space to picnic—at tables or on the grass.
✚ Off map to southeast ✉ 31 Darling Street, Abbotsbury ☎ 9748 2222 ⏰ Daily 9–5 🚆 Fairfield

CLOUD 9 BALLOON FLIGHTS

An adventurous way to view Sydney is from the air. Take a hot-air balloon flight and follow it with a champagne breakfast.
✚ Off map to northeast ✉ Annangrove ☎ 9679 2899 ⏰ Daily at dawn 🚆 Parramatta

HARBOUR JET

Extreme harbour tours by jet boat. A choice of the 35-minute Jet Blast tour (includes 270-degree spins and power brake stops) or the slightly more sedate 50-minute Sydney Harbour Adventure. Photo opportunities and music.
✚ G6 ✉ 113a Harbourside Centre, Darling Harbour ☎ 1300 887 373 ⏰ Daily 🚌 Convention

HAYDEN ORPHEUM PICTURE PALACE

Far more than just a cinema, the Orpheum is worth a visit for its wonderful art-deco interior and old-fashioned touches—such as Wurlitzer organ music at some film sessions.
✚ L1 ✉ 380 Military Road, Cremorne ☎ 9908 4344 ⏰ Daily 🚌 178, 180, 182, 247

SHARK DIVE EXTREME

Dive safely and view sharks, stingrays and sea turtles up close in an aquarium environment.
✚ Off map to northeast ✉ West Esplanade, Manly ☎ 8251 7878 ⏰ Daily ⛴ Manly

WHITEWATER RAFTING

Located at the foot of the Blue Mountains, on the site of the Olympic kayaking events, this rafting and kayaking venue offers whitewater fun and thrills. Reservations essential.
✚ Off map to west ✉ McCarthy's Lane, Cranebrook ☎ 4730 4333 ⏰ Daily 9–5 🚆 Penrith Station

THE MOVIE SCENE

The main complexes are on George Street, south of Bathurst Street and at 232 Pitt Street. Alternative cinema include the Dendy at Martin Place and 624 George Street; both have bars, while the Martin Place venue offers a bistro and specialist film-buff shop. Less mainstream foreign and offbeat films are also screened at the Academy Twin, 3a Oxford Street, Paddington. For details, see the *Sydney Morning Herald*.

FOX STUDIOS SHOPPING CENTRE

This complex of cinemas, restaurants, shops and markets is Sydney's latest entertainment and dining hotspot. For kids there is Lollipops, a multi-level fun complex with mazes, tunnels, ball pits and adventure playgrounds.
✚ L8 ✉ Lang Road, Moore Park ☎ 9383 4333; www.foxstudios.com.au ⏰ Daily 10am–late; closed 25 Dec 🚌 372, 377, 390, 399

Luxury Hotels

PRICES

The following price guide for hotels is shown in Australian dollars. This is what you may expect to pay per room per night regardless of single or double occupancy:

Luxury   more than $250
Mid-Range up to $250
Budget   up to $100

It is always worth asking when you make your reservation whether any special deals are available. There are also many economical self-catering serviced apartments, while reasonably priced guesthouses and hostels are plentiful. Sydney's major hotel areas are The Rocks, the city centre, Kings Cross and North Sydney.

FOUR SEASONS HOTEL

Situated between the city centre and The Rocks, this is one of Australia's better hotels, with the city's largest hotel pool. Its Kable's restaurant offers fine dining. 531 rooms.
✚ bii; J5 ✉ 199 George Street ☎ 9238 0000; fax 9251 2851; www.fourseasons.com 🚉 Circular Quay

HOTEL INTER-CONTINENTAL SYDNEY

Close to the Botanic Gardens and The Rocks, this 503-room hotel is based on the historic 1851 Treasury Building
✚ cii; K5 ✉ 117 Macquarie Street ☎ 9253 9000; fax 9240 1240; www.intercontinental.com 🚉 Circular Quay

FOUR POINTS SHERATON

A glossy, deluxe hotel with 645 rooms, overlooking Darling Harbour. It blends modern design with historic buildings, including the 1850s Dundee Arms Pub.
✚ aiii; J6 ✉ Corner of Sussex and King streets ☎ 9290 4000; fax 9299 3340; www.fourpoints.com/sydney 🚉 Monorail to Darling Park

PARK HYATT SYDNEY

In terms of harbourside location, this hotel with 158 rooms including suites, has it all, plus direct views to the Harbour Bridge and Opera House. Elegant restaurant.
✚ J4 ✉ 7 Hickson Road, The Rocks ☎ 9256 1555; fax 9256 1355; www.hyatt.com 🚉 Circular Quay

SHANGRI-LA HOTEL SYDNEY

One of Sydney's newest hotels, offering wonderful views over the harbour. There are 10 dining and entertainment facilities and the cocktail bar has superb panoramic views for just the price of a drink. A total of 561 rooms.
✚ aiii; J5 🔲 176 Cumberland Street, The Rocks ☎ 9250 6000; fax 9250 6250; www.shangri-la.com 🚉 Circular Quay

SHERATON ON THE PARK

One of the Sheraton group's élite Luxury Collection,this magnificent central hotel has a grand three-storey lobby and a fine restaurant. Excellent views. 557 rooms.
✚ biv; J6 ✉ 161 Elizabeth Street ☎ 9286 6000; fax 9286 6686; www.sheraton.com/sydney 🚉 St. James

THE WESTIN SYDNEY

Part of the old Sydney GPO, this international hotel with 416 rooms, has lavish facilities and features a section with 'heritage' rooms.
✚ biii; J5 ✉ 1 Martin Place ☎ 8223 1111; fax 8223 1222; www. westin.com.au 🚉 Circular Quay

W SYDNEY

Sydney's hippest hotel is part of an old shipping wharf close to the Royal Botanic Gardens. 104 rooms.
✚ diii; K6 ✉ 5 Cowper Street, Woolloomooloo ☎ 9331 9000; fax 9331 9031; www.whotels.com 🚍 311

Mid-Range Hotels & Apartments

CASTLEREAGH HOTEL

Very central and good value, featuring a finely restored dining room. All 82 rooms have private bathrooms.

➕ biv; J6 ✉ 169 Castlereagh Street ☎ 9284 1000; fax 9284 1999; www.thecastlereagh.net.au
🚇 Town Hall

HUGHENDEN BOUTIQUE HOTEL

Located in the heart of Paddington, this Victorian manor boutique hotel offers 36 ensuite rooms.

➕ M8 ✉ 14 Queen Street, Woollahra ☎ 9363 4863; fax 9362 0398; www.hughendenhotel.com.au 🚌 378, 380

KIRKETON BOUTIQUE HOTEL

This boutique designer hotel is stylish and hip and has 40 rooms. Good restaurant.

➕ K7 ✉ 229 Darlinghurst Road, Darlinghurst ☎ 9332 2011; fax 9332 2499; www.kirketon.com.au 🚇 Kings Cross

MORGANS OF SYDNEY

The 26 spacious suites are elegantly furnished and have queen-sized beds. Good views from the roof-top deck.

➕ K6 ✉ 304 Victoria Street, Darlinghurst ☎ 9360 7955; fax 9360 9217; www.morganshotel.com.au 🚇 Kings Cross

OAKFORD APARTMENTS

These comfortable self-contained apartments offer fully equipped kitchens, private balconies and pleasant water views. 48 rooms plus a swimming pool.

➕ G8 ✉ 23–33 Missenden Road, Camperdown ☎ 9557 6100; www.oakford.com
🚌 412, 413, 436, 438

RAVESI'S ON BONDI BEACH

This boutique hotel has just 16 rooms and suites, overlooking Bondi Beach. The restaurant and cocktail bar are excellent and the hotel is tastefully decorated and furnished.

➕ Off map to east ✉ 118 Campbell Parade, Bondi Beach ☎ 9365 4422; fax 9365 1481; www.ravesis.com.au
🚌 380, 382

VICTORIA COURT HOTEL SYDNEY

This charming 1881-built Victorian guesthouse, pleasantly situated on a leafy avenue in Potts Point, is a member of the Historic Hotels of Australia network. Very comfortable and makes for an atmospheric stay. 25 rooms.

➕ div; L6 ✉ 122 Victoria Street, Potts Point ☎ 9357 3200; fax 9357 7606; www.victoriacourt.com.au
🚇 Kings Cross

THE YORK APARTMENT HOTEL

This apartment hotel is located near Darling Harbour, and has 140 comfortable one-bedroom apartments with maid service. Each has a kitchen, balcony and separate dining room.

➕ aiii; J6 ✉ 5 York Street ☎ 9210 5000; fax 9290 1487; www.theyorkapartments.com.au
🚇 Wynyard

APARTMENTS

Apartment-style hotels in Sydney generally fall into the mid-range price category. These so-called serviced apartments vary from one to three bedrooms, with separate dining areas and kitchens or kitchenettes. Many are large enough for families or small groups.

87

Budget Hotels & Guesthouses

BUDGET ACCOMMODATION

In addition to these budget hotels, Sydney has dozens of backpackers' lodges. Prices start at $15 per night and many establishments offer reduced rates for long stays. Accommodation varies from private rooms to dormitories and the best backpacker areas are Kings Cross, inner-west Glebe and beach suburbs such as Bondi and Coogee. Another budget option is staying in a 'hotel'. In Australia, the word hotel, confusingly, has two meanings: the conventional hotel and a pub with a few bedrooms. More details can be obtained from the NSW Travel Centre (☎ 9231 4444).

AARONS HOTEL SYDNEY

Better-than-average accommodation, near Darling Harbour, with 24-hour reception services. Restaurant and bar. 93 rooms.

➕ J7 ✉ 37 Ultimo Road, Haymarket ☎ 1800 101 100; fax 9281 2666; www.aaronshotel. com.au 🚇 Central

AUSTRALIAN SUNRISE LODGE

Good choice of single or double rooms, most with private balcony and bathrooms. Well located in the vibrant suburb of Newtown. 22 rooms.

➕ Off map to west ✉ 485 King Street, Newtown ☎ 9550 4999; fax 9550 4457 🚌 422 🚇 Newtown

BONDI BEACHOUSE YHA

Just a 20-minute bus ride to either the airport or CBD, this popular 50-room hostel includes double rooms with private bath.

➕ Off map to east ✉ 63 Fletcher Street, Bondi Beach ☎ 9365 2088; www.bondibeachouse.com.au 🚌 380, 382

CREMORNE POINT MANOR

Located on the north shore a few minutes by ferry from the city, this 30-room manor house provides kitchens, laundry service and a continental breakfast on request.

➕ L3 ✉ 6 Cremorne Road, Cremorne Point ☎ 9953 7899; fax 9904 1265; www.cremornepointmanor.com.au 🚢 Cremorne Point

MANLY BEACH RESORT

This resort offers double, twin and family rooms—40 in all—a swimming pool and good facilities. A scenic ferry ride away from the city.

➕ Off map to northeast ✉ 6 Carlton Street, Manly ☎ 9977 4188; fax 9977 0524; www.manlyview.com.au 🚢 Manly

NOAH'S ON BONDI

Popular budget choice with shared facilities. Billiard table, internet and TV room. 74 rooms.

➕ Off map to east ✉ 2 Campbell Parade, Bondi Beach ☎ 9365 7100; fax 9365 7644; www.totaltravel.com.au 🚌 380, 382, 389

SYDNEY CENTRAL YHA

Near Central station, it's excellent for back-packers . You don't need a hostel card to stay here. 140 rooms.

➕ J7 ✉ Corner of Pitt Street and Rawson Place ☎ 9281 9111; fax 9281 9199; www.yha.org.au 🚇 Central

VULCAN HOTEL

This stylish, heritage-listed 30-room hotel, just minutes from Darling Harbour, has a licensed bar/café and internet access.

➕ H6 ✉ 500 Wattle Street, Ultimo ☎ 9211 3283; fax 9212 7439; www.vulcanhotel.com.au 🚇 Central

Y ON THE PARK

On edge of the city, this spotless and popular hostel has 127 rooms.

➕ K7 ✉ 5–11 Wentworth Avenue ☎ 9264 2451; fax 9285 6288; www.ywca-sydney.com.au 🚇 Museum

SYDNEY
travel facts

ESSENTIAL FACTS

Customs regulations

- Visitors aged 18 or over may bring in 250 cigarettes or 250g of tobacco or cigars; 2.25 litres of alcohol; plus other dutiable goods to the value of $900 per person.
- There is no limit on money imported for personal use, although amounts in excess of $10,000 or its equivalent must be declared on arrival.
- Animals are subject to quarantine, and goods of plant or animal origin must be declared on arrival. It is forbidden to bring in food.
- Drugs smuggling is treated very seriously and harshly, and import-ing firearms and products from endangered species is illegal or restricted.

Electricity

- The electricity supply in Australia is 230–250 volts AC. Three-flat-pin plugs are the standard (although note that they are unlike British plugs).
- Hotels provide standard 110-volt and 240-volt shaver sockets.

Etiquette

- Smoking is prohibited on public transport (including inside airport terminals), in restaurants, cinemas, theatres and most shops and shopping malls.
- Tipping (normally 10 per cent) is expected only in restaurants where service charges are not added to bills. Tipping taxi-drivers and hotel staff is optional.

Lavatories

- Free lavatories are found in parks, public places, galleries and museums, department stores and bus and train stations.

Money matters

- Currency exchanges at hotels, some shops, tourist centres and outlets such as American Express and Thomas Cook are open outside banking hours. Airport exchange facilities are open daily 5.30am–11pm. You can obtain cash from 24-hour cash machines (ATMs) throughout the city and country.
- Major credit cards (American Express, Visa and MasterCard) are widely accepted.
- A 10 per cent goods and services tax is automatically added to your purchases, however if you buy goods valued at $300 or more from any one supplier you can claim the tax back from the designated booths at Sydney Airport.

Opening hours

- Shops: generally Mon–Fri 9–5.30, Sat 9–4. Late-night shopping until 9 on Thu. Large stores open Sun until 4. Suburban corner shops often open daily 8–8 or later.
- Post offices: Mon–Fri 9–5. Sydney GPO hours are Mon–Fri 8.15–5.30, Sat 8.30–noon.
- Banks: Mon–Thu 9.30–4, Fri 9.30–5. City head-office banks open Mon–Fri 8.15–5.

Places of worship

- Anglican: St. Andrew's Cathedral ✉ Sydney Square, George Street
- Roman Catholic: St. Mary's Cathedral ✉ College Street
- Presbyterian: Scots Church ✉ 44 Margaret Street
- Baptist: Central Baptist Church ✉ 619 George Street
- Interdenominational: Wayside Chapel ✉ 29 Hughes Street, Kings Cross
- Jewish: The Great Synagogue ✉ 166 Castlereagh Street
- Buddhist: Buddhist Centre

☎ 9929 8643
- Muslim: Sydney Mosque
  ✉ 13 John Street, Erskineville

Public holidays
- 1 Jan, 26 Jan (Australia Day), Good Fri, Easter Mon, 25 Apr (Anzac Day), 2nd Mon in Jun (Queen's birthday), 1st Mon in Aug (NSW; banks only), 1st Mon in Oct (Labor Day: NSW state holiday), 25–26 Dec.
- School summer holidays are mid-December to late January. As a result transport and tourist facilities are very busy and accommodation is heavily reserved at this time.

Tourist information
- Phone information services: Traveller Accommodation Service ☎ 9669 5111 Sydney Information Line ☎ 9911 7700
- Sydney's Visitor Centre ✉ 106 George Street, The Rocks ☎ 9255 1788 🕐 Mon–Fri 9–5 offers general information as well as maps and accommodation listings.
- Tourism New South Wales ☎ 13 2077; www.visitnsw.com
- Australian Tourist Commission offices outside Australia: UK ✉ 10–18 Putney Hill, London, SW15 6AA ☎ 020 8780 2229 USA ✉ 2049 Century Park East Suite 1920, Los Angeles, CA 90067 ☎ 310/229–4870

GETTING AROUND

- For timetable and ticket information (buses, ferries and Cityrail trains) ☎ 13 1500 🕐 Daily 6am–10pm
- Monorail information ☎ 8584 5288
- Countrylink (out of town) train information ☎ 13 2232

Monorail
- Use the monorail for the Sydney Aquarium, National Maritime Museum and Powerhouse Museum.
- The monorail runs every few minutes Mon–Thu 7am–9.45pm, Fri, Sat 7am–11.45, Sun 8am–9.45pm. You can buy an economical all-day pass.

Taxis and water taxis
- Cabs are abundant and fares are reasonable by world standards.
- Main operators include: Legion Cabs ☎ 13 1451; Taxis Combined Services ☎ 8332 8888; Premier Cabs ☎ 13 1017; RSL Cabs ☎ 13 2211
- Taxis for people with disabilities ☎ 9339 0200
- Water taxis: Yellow Water Taxis ☎ 9299 1099

Trains
- Sydney's inner-city rail services include the City Circle (Central, Town Hall, Wynyard, Circular Quay, St. James and Museum) and the Eastern Suburbs Line, which runs from Central to Town Hall, Martin Place, Kings Cross, Edgecliff and Bondi Junction.

Tickets
- The Sydneypass, valid for three, five or seven days, includes the Airport Express bus, cruises, the Explorer buses and unlimited travel on the regular state-operated bus and ferry services.
- Train: Off-peak tickets (for travel at weekends and after 9am at weekdays) represent a 45 per cent saving. A Cityhopper pass allows travel on the inner-city rail service all day for a very reasonable price. Other Travelpasses include rail, bus and ferry travel.
- Buses: Bustripper passes allow

unlimited travel all day on the bus network; a budget Travelten ticket is valid for 10 journeys. The red Sydney Explorer and blue Bondi & Bay Explorer services operate to the city's most important sights at regular intervals daily 9am–6pm. Tickets offer all day travel and the option of leaving and reboarding the buses at will.

- Ferries: A Ferrytravel ticket offers a considerable saving for 10 journeys. Travelpasses also permit a combination of bus, ferry and train travel. There are also special ferry travel/entrance passes to attractions such as Taronga Zoo, the Aquarium and Oceanworld.
- For more information on getting around ➤ 6–7.

DRIVING & CAR RENTAL

Driving

- Driving is on the left and overtaking traffic (which has the right of way) is on the right. This, however, may not be immediately obvious on multi-lane highways, where the preference seems to be to stay in the right-hand lane. On some stretches of winding roads, lay-bys are provided to be used by slow traffic to enable other drivers to overtake.
- Take special care when driving on unsurfaced roads; they are best avoided. Also, avoid driving in the country at night; and beware of stray animals on motorways at dawn and dusk.
- Some road signs are peculiar to Australia, but most will be immediately understandable to visitors.
- Full details of Australia's road rules are available at www.aaa.asn.au

- Speed limits are 50/60kph (31/37mph) in urban areas and 100/110kph (62/68mph) elsewhere unless indicated.
- Seatbelts must be worn in front and back seats.
- Fuel (unleaded and super unleaded) is sold by the litre; gas stations are numerous but may have restricted weekend opening hours.
- The legal limit for alcohol is 0.05 percent blood alcohol level.

Car rental

- Renting a car may be necessary for some of the out-of-town trips within this book. You must be over 21. Compulsory third-party insurance is included in rental prices, which are on average $60–$80 per day. Visitors must have an international driving licence or a valid overseas driving licence (with a translation if it is not in English).
- Major Sydney car-rental companies:
  Avis ☎ 13 6333; Budget ☎ 13 2727; Hertz ☎ 13 3039

MEDIA & COMMUNICATIONS

Newspapers & magazines

- The main national newspaper is *The Australian*.
- The major city newspaper is the *Sydney Morning Herald*.
- The weekly *Bulletin Newsweek* is Australia's answer to *Time*.

Postal services

- Larger post offices provide services such as aerograms, fax facilities and e-mail.
- Stamps can also be purchased from hotels, and from some newsstands and souvenir shops.
- Postage information ☎ 13 1317

Telephones

- Public telephones are found at phone booths, post offices, hotels, service stations, shops, rail and bus stations and cafés. There is a 24-hour telephone centre ✉ 100 King Street. Local calls cost 40¢ for unlimited time (20¢ and 10¢ coins can be used).
- Long-distance calls within Australia, known as STD, vary in price, but you should have a good supply of 50¢ and $1 coins. Calls are less expensive after 6pm and all day Sunday.
- Operator assistance and directory assistance ☎ 1234
- Reverse-charge calls ☎ 12 550
- Phonecards come in values of $2 to $20; credit cards can also be used from some (silver) phones.
- For international (IDD) calls (can be made from some public phones) dial 0011 followed by the country codes: US and Canada 1; UK 44; France 33; Germany 49.
- To call Australia from the US dial 011 61; from the UK dial 00 61, then drop the initial zero from the area code.
- To call a Sydney number from outside the metropolitan area, use the prefix 02.

EMERGENCIES

Consulates

- Canada ☎ 9364 3000
- France ☎ 9261 5779
- Germany ☎ 9328 7733
- UK ☎ 9247 7521
- USA ☎ 9373 9200

Emergency phone numbers

- Police, ambulance or fire ☎ 000 (24 hours). All calls for these services are free.
- Dental, pharmaceutical, personal, or other: See the front of the A–K

volume of the Sydney White Pages telephone book.

Medical treatment

- Medical, dental and ambulance services are excellent but costly.
- Doctors and dentists are readily available and there are many medical centres where appointments are not necessary.
- Hotel Doctor ☎ 9962 6000 ⏰ Daily 7am–11pm (applies only to CBD hotels)

Medicines

- You may bring in prescribed medications. Keep them in the original containers and bring a copy of your doctor's prescription to avoid problems at customs.

Sensible precautions

- Report theft or any other incident to your hotel and/or the police as soon as possible. If your travellers' cheques are stolen, advise the relevant organization.
- The non-emergency, police inquiries number is ☎ 9281 0000
- Sydney's police wear blue uniforms and a peaked cap. They are generally helpful and polite.
- Tap water is safe to drink; the only medical problems you are likely to experience are sunburn and mosquito bites.
- If you burn easily, generously apply sun block SPF15+, wear sunglasses, a broad-brimmed hat and long sleeves, and avoid the summer sun from 11 to 3.
- Dangerous currents and marine stingers can cause problems in the sea in summer, so take notice of lifeguards and any beach signs.
- Women are generally safe in Sydney, but walking alone in parks or on beaches at night and traveling alone on trains out of the central city area is not recommended.

Index

CityPack
Sydney *Top 25*

ABOUT THE AUTHOR

Anne Matthews developed a passion for Australia at a time when 'Down Under' was utterly unfashionable. She emigrated to Sydney from England in 1979 and spent seven years working in the adventure travel industry, including an extended period of living in India and Nepal. After returning to Sydney in 1986, Anne became a travel writer and photographer, specializing in guidebooks and brochures.

WRITTEN BY   Anne Matthews
EDITION REVISER AND CONTRIBUTIONS TO 'LIVING SYDNEY'   Rod Ritchie
MANAGING EDITORS   Apostrophe S Limited
COVER DESIGN   Tigist Getachew, Fabrizio La Rocca

A CIP catalogue record for this book is available from the British Library.

ISBN-10: 0-7495-3931-3
ISBN-13: 978-0-7495-3931-3

The contents of this publication are believed correct at the time of printing. Nevertheless, the publishers cannot be held responsible for any errors or omissions or for changes in the details given in this guide or for the consequences of any reliance on the information provided by the same. This does not affect your statutory rights. Assessments of attractions, hotels, restaurants and so forth are based upon the author's own personal experience and, therefore, descriptions given in this guide necessarily contain an element of subjective opinion which may not reflect the publishers' opinion or dictate a reader's own experiences on another occasion. We have tried to ensure accuracy in this guide, but things do change and we would be grateful if readers would advise us of any inaccuracies they may encounter.

Published by AA Publishing, a trading name of Automobile Association Developments Limited, whose registered office is Fanum House, Basing View, Basingstoke, Hampshire, RG21 4EA. Registered number 1878835).

© **AUTOMOBILE ASSOCIATION DEVELOPMENTS LIMITED 1996, 1998, 2000, 2004, 2006**
First published 1996. Reprinted 1997. Revised second edition 1998. Reprinted Jan 1999. Revised third edition 2000. Reprinted, Sep 2001, Aug 2002. Revised fourth edition 2004. Reprinted Mar 2005. **Reprinted Jan 2006. Information verified and updated.**
Reprinted June 2007

Colour separation by Daylight Colour Art Pte Ltd, Singapore
Printed and bound by Hang Tai D&P Limited, Hong Kong

ACKNOWLEDGEMENTS
The Automobile Association would like to thank the following photographers, libraries and associations for their assistance in the preparation of this title.
The Art Gallery of NSW 45b; Australian National Maritime Museum 39; Australian Tourist Commission 26b, 36b, 42b, 43b, 57; Bridgeclimb 16/17; Historic Houses Trust of New South Wales 49, 54, 55; Lone Pine Koala Sanctuary 59; A Matthews 30, 42, 44; Museum of Contemporary Art 42t; Museum of Sydney 46t, 46b; Office of the Prime Minister of Australian 17r; Pictures Colour Library 89t; Stockbyte 5. The remaining photographs are held in the Association's own library (AA WORLD TRAVEL LIBRARY) and were taken by Mike Langford, with the exception of; Adrian Baker front cover: kangaroos, 27t, 29t, 31t, 31b, 34, 38, 40, 48t, 48b, 62; Steve Day 1b, 17c, 21, 29b, 50; Paul Kenward 20l, 22c, 26t, 27b, 29t, 28, 32t, 32b, 33, 35, 36t, 37t, 37b, 43t, 45t, 47, 52, 56, 60, 61, 89b.

A03484
Maps © Automobile Association Developments Limited 2006
Fold out map © MAIRDUMONT / Falk Verlag 2007
Transport map © Communicarta Ltd, UK

TITLES IN THE CITYPACK SERIES

• Amsterdam • Bangkok • Barcelona • Beijing • Berlin • Boston • Brussels & Bruges •
• Chicago • Dublin • Edinburgh • Florence • Hong Kong • Istanbul • Las Vegas • Lisbon •
• Ljubljana • London • Los Angeles • Madrid • Melbourne • Miami • Montréal • Munich •
• New York • Orlando • Paris • Prague • Rome • San Francisco • Seattle • Shanghai •
• Singapore • Sydney • Tokyo • Toronto • Venice • Vienna • Washington DC •